SEATED IN HEAVENLY PLACES

Ana Méndez Ferrell

International

E & A INTERNATIONAL

Seated In Heavenly Places
4th Printing

Cover design:
Ruben Mariaca Asport, areyou_ben@hotmail.com

Interior design:
*osprey*design

Printing:
Total Printing Systems

Category:
Apostolic Reformation

All scripture quotations unless otherwise indicated are taken from the King James Version

Publisher:
E & A INTERNATIONAL
P.O. Box 3418
Ponte Vedra Florida 32004
www.voiceofthelight.com

ISBN: 1-933163-07-0

Dedication

I dedicate this book to my beloved heavenly Father, to Jesus Christ, and to the Holy Spirit, through whose favor and grace I received the revelations herein described. I also dedicate it to my precious family, my husband, Emerson, and my children, Ana, Pedro and Jordan.

Appreciation

I want to express my deepest thanks to my spiritual parents, my pastors and apostles, Rony and Lia Chaves, to my apostles from the United States, Peter and Doris Wagner, who have diligently watched over my ministry in Jesus Christ. I would also like to thank all of my intercessors who have fought the good fight together with me.

Contents

Introduction

We have entered a new millennium, and with it into the most wonderful and exciting era of the Church. God is bringing upon the earth amazing waves of anointing and revelation with the mission of bringing about a powerful, apostolic reformation.

A few years ago, just before the turn of the century, I began to hear a commotion in the heavens. It was something continuous that would not let me sleep. The voice of God shouted loudly, "Reformation, behold I come."

The Lord began to shake my life, to remove everything that could be removed or shaken, so that only the unshakeable would remain. My life, my way of seeing things, everything began to be transformed into something new and powerful.

The Holy Spirit prompted me to reread the scriptures, to leave behind my old patterns and paradigms. He was forming a new wineskin and pouring out a new wine that would change my entire way of thinking.

I began to have extraordinary experiences in the Spirit. I have been taken to heaven many times to see and understand things that have been hidden for generations but that God wants to reveal to us.

For centuries creation has groaned to see the glorious manifestation of the sons of God. And its groans have been heard! A new apostolic and prophetic generation is rising up all over the world, an ever-advancing army that cannot be stopped, a people of God who will move in the power of the greatest signs and wonders in history. The glory of Jehovah will truly be seen in them, and kings and the powerful men of the earth will run to them in order to be with Jesus.

God is calling us to understand the deep things of His Kingdom, to enter into spiritual levels we never before dreamed of or imagined. God is calling us to change our earthly, human way of thinking with its limited levels of faith. He wants to convert us into real PEOPLE OF THE KINGDOM, sons of God who the devil cannot stop, or close doors to, a people with the dominion and authority of God to govern the earth with Christ.

Jesus came to restore that which was lost, and one of the main things that mankind lost was reigning with God on earth.

And God blessed them, and God said unto them, Be fruitful, and multiply, and replenish the earth, and subdue it: and have dominion over the fish of the sea, and over the fowl of the air, and over every living thing that moveth upon the earth.

—*Genesis 1:28*

And the Bible also says, speaking about the victory of Jesus Christ and of His Church:

And the kingdom and dominion, and the greatness of the kingdom under the whole heaven, shall be given to the people of the saints of the Most High, whose kingdom is an everlasting kingdom, and all dominions shall serve and obey him.

—*Daniel 7:27*

These lines are part of the fruit of the transformation that He has made in my life, in order to teach us to have dominion and authority in the invisible world, and to change every circumstance that opposes the kingdom of God.

This is a book of REFORMATION, as much internally as in paradigms. It is a book that will challenge the deepest parts of your being, so that God can take you and seat you with Him on his throne. You will learn that there is a big difference between saying, "I am seated with Jesus on His throne," and knowing without a doubt that He has taken you by the hand and has seated you there, knowing that you are reigning with Him.

To him that overcometh will I grant to sit with me in my throne, even as I also overcame, and am set down with my Father in his throne.

—*Revelation 3:21*

These pages will also cause you to open yourself and to understand the spiritual realm, to be able to penetrate the most beautiful places in the dimensions of the Spirit. They will allow you to see and to know God face to face, not when you die, but here and now.

You will discover truths that will shake you and will confront in its entirety the way you see things. Veils will fall that you never knew existed. This will allow the Kingdom of God to open before you in an extraordinary way.

You were chosen before the foundation of the world to be part of the most glorious era of the Church. Ever since you were born, your spirit was already sealed with the stamp of glory. The word says:

> Ye have not chosen me, but I HAVE CHOSEN YOU...
>
> —*John 15:16*

And He chose us with a purpose:

> ...That ye should go and bring forth fruit, and that your fruit should remain; that whatsoever ye shall ask of the Father in my name, he may give it you.
>
> —*John 15:16*

If you open your heart and permit the Spirit to give testimony of what is written here, your life will be radically transformed.

I am sharing here a few of the most precious experiences that I have had with God. Upon reading them you will realize that the language that I use is different from what you are used to hearing or reading; and I did it this way so that you too would desire to enter into the dimensions that God has prepared for you. All I can promise you is that the Lord is desiring to reveal himself in your life and that he that searches, finds, and he that knocks, it will be opened to him. And whoever comes to Him, Jesus will not cast out.

Jesus is coming and He reveals himself in direct proportion to the amount of hunger and thirst that we have for Him and His Kingdom. Someone once said, "Show me your hunger with your boldness. Show me your searching with your perseverance, and then I will believe that you will find him."

My prayer upon writing this book is that it creates such a hunger in you to know God and to possess his Kingdom, that you won't stop until everything that is written in this book is fulfilled in your life.

1

CHRIST, THE APOSTLE, REVEALED

During the last ten years of the past century and in the beginning of this century, we saw a very important flourishing of the prophetic move. The Holy Spirit is revealing Christ in a marvelous way.

New torrents of anointing and of the knowledge of God have been descending upon the Church. And there is a sense of dissatisfaction and a passion in the true people of God that the Lord himself is using to carry us to glorious levels that no other generation has experienced.

Among the new things that are occurring is the rebirth of the apostolic move. This new move is being talked about in all circles. God is raising up great men and women with a different anointing, an apostolic anointing, so that His designs will be accomplished on the earth.

These words bring conflict in some people. This is due to the erroneous way in which the concept of apostle has been handled by many, using it as a means by which to exercise authority over others in order to subjugate them under their control. That is why I am asking you to lay aside all preconceived ideas of what "apostolic" is and open your spirit to a fresh revelation from heaven.

The first thing we need to understand is that the "apostolic" is not only one of the five ministries mentioned in the fourth chapter of the epistle to the Ephesians, but a manifestation of Christ on the earth.

Let me go to the root of all this. In order to understand the "apostolic," it is necessary to first understand the prophetic move, since the one assists the other.

The scripture says in Revelation 19:10 that the Spirit of prophecy is the testimony of Jesus. This means that the manifestation of the prophetic is the revelation of all that Jesus is. The very essence of prophecy does not consist of telling each other about the beautiful things that God has for us, but its objective is to reveal the multiple facts of Christ Himself.

The foundation of the Church, based on the apostles and prophets, is the revelation of Christ. The glorious Church that Jesus is raising up is not founded on doctrines, but on revelation.

When the prophetic move is flowing, with the move surges an impressive wave of the intimate knowledge of Jesus. It also opens spiritual dimensions so we can enter into a deep understanding of the different levels of the Kingdom of God that He wants to show us.

The prophetic anointing is going to permit us to see and understand the spiritual world. It is going to give us the power to modify and transform this invisible realm, which is over everything that surrounds us, in order to establish the Kingdom of the Almighty.

The prophetic is that which permits us to discover and see the designs of God in the heavens and where we have the authority to make proclamations and symbolic acts that establish the will of God in the celestial regions. It is this anointing that produces the power to straighten the crooked path, bring low the high mountains, exalt the valleys, and prepare the way of the Lord. In addition, it is this anointing that is going to give birth to the powerful revelation of Christ, "the Apostle."

When He presents Himself as apostle, He will bring new levels of divine power and government that are going to facilitate the establishment of God's purposes and structures in the natural world. It is the supernatural ability that God gives to bring things from the invisible realm to the visible.

This is not just God pointing out which ministries are apostolic ministries, which of course He will do. It is not instructions as to how to set up a denomination either or a series of regulations by which to supervise churches. No!

It is a manifestation of Christ that affects the whole earth. It will change the course of the Church towards the greatest dimensions of glory. It will touch all believers, and it will powerfully fall upon unbelievers to draw them towards the Kingdom of God.

To understand the apostolic is to understand a new and specific revelation of Christ, with the whole gamut of characteristics of which it is comprised.

Pastors will begin to move under this anointing, without this necessarily meaning that they are apostles. They will be pastors under a new dimension of power. They will become new wineskins into which God will pour His new wine in a most glorious way. The same will happen to evangelists, teachers and prophets.

Praying and worshipping will be transformed and taken to amazing heights. The true order of God will begin to manifest itself in everything. The will of God will be done on earth as it is in heaven. As a consequence, the greatest power of God will descend upon the Church so that the Kingdom of God will be seen flowing in all of its greatness.

This will bring with it strong shakings in methods and human doctrines that have so failed in bringing the glory of God to the earth and in bringing in the great harvest. In this move, God will align his people with his justice and with his Righteousness.

What we will see in the churches will no longer be the eloquence of man, nor the plans and routines of well-intentioned pastors, but we will see His glory in the open heavens. This will affect the way in which one preaches and worships; everything human will come down so that only the celestial will remain.

The heavens will literally invade the services with wonderful, angelic visitations and also in the every day life of the believers because the Holy Spirit will be uniting the heavens and the earth as it is written:

Having made known unto us the mystery of his will, according to his good pleasure which he hath purposed in himself:

That in the dispensation of the fullness of times he might gather together in one all things in Christ, both which are in heaven, and which are on earth; even in him:

—*Ephesians 1:9-10*

The most wonderful thing is that it already has begun. This anointing is coming to unite.

It will join the two dimensions, the natural and the spiritual. It will unite the body of Christ. It will unite parents and children. It will bring reconciliation among the generations. Parents will rejoice over the success of their children. Children will honor their parents. And I am speaking not only in the natural sense, but also in the spiritual sense. The internal government of the Church will be of true parents who motivate and protect their children.

The apostolic is the redemptive manifestation of everything. Everything that touches this anointing brings redemption. The Word says:

For it pleased the Father that in him should all fullness dwell;

And, having made peace through the blood of his cross, by him to reconcile all things unto himself; by him, I say, whether they be things in earth, or things in heaven.

—*Colossians 1:19-20*

This means that we are going to see all of the designs and purposes of God made reality in our lives. We will see how we were conceived. We will see the redemption of the original purposes that God had when He created the nations and that were perverted by the devil. The nations will enter into a new light.

When heaven manifests itself on earth, we are going to see the government of God established upon the earth. God will choose those who will reign with Him. And the important decisions in a nation will not be made by unbelievers, but by the children of God. We will see constitutions change. Political parties that have served the designs of the devil will come down totally.

The time has come when we will govern with Jesus. I am not only referring to Christians in politics, even though this will happen and in a great way. I am referring to a spiritual government that determines the course and the decisions of a natural government, as in the case of Rees Howells, who with his team from his prayer room, brought the defeat of Hitler.

The children of God in this new apostolic generation will open doors of hidden treasures. Fountains of riches not yet discovered will come to light. This will occur because the true prophets and apostles will declare it in the power of the Spirit and they will bring these treasures from the invisible to the visible.

The designs of God will be established upon the earth. The Church will leave its four walls in order to manifest the glory and power of God in every sphere of society.

The river that flows from the temple of God in the heavens, will flood the streets of the cities with an army of believers who are "living messages," that will pour out the love and the power of the Father wherever they go.

The word will come to pass that says,

Arise, shine; for thy light is come, and the glory of the LORD is risen upon thee.

For, behold, the darkness shall cover the earth, and gross darkness the people: but the LORD shall arise upon thee, and his glory shall be seen upon thee.

—*Isaiah 60:1-2*

The river will touch millions because it is laden with life and fruit, and it will bring healing to the nations.

We will see apostles spring forth in the financial world; men and women full of the glory of God and divine zeal, who will attract to themselves the riches of the nations. They will be true economic pillars, with generous and pure hearts, who will help the needy and will establish the Kingdom of God. They will be messengers of the Lord (apostles) in order to put into the hands of the true servants of the Most High the necessary funds to take the gospel to every creature.

We are going to see the raising up of ministries of powerful women. We will see young people move in extraordinary power and revelation.

Do you realize that this goes a lot further than the apostolic concept of the last century that limited itself to pastors giving a covering to other pastors? The revelation of the magnitude of what this move means had not yet been received.

The Essence of the Apostolic Spirit

In this redemptive anointing of Christ, we are going to observe the revelation of His light as never before. Light is the vehicle that brings redemption from heaven to earth.

Let's take Genesis as a type that will help us understand how He will restore all things. We see in this book how the earth was without form and void. The waters covered the face of the deep, and the Spirit of God moved over the face of the waters. It is at this moment that the manifestation of "Christ-Apostles" appears for the first time.

God proclaims light into existence. This light, which is not the light of the sun, is the Lord himself. Light represents what is revealed, that which permits one to see where before one could not see.

The first thing that the light does is it sets boundaries around darkness. Later comes the redemption of the earth. First darkness is put in its place. Then can come restoration and the creation of all things.

For there to be creation, in order for the invisible to come to the visible plane, first what is out of order must be restored to order.

Order, which is a characteristic of the apostolic move, first of all, is going to separate what is in chaos so that each part finds its proper place.

We see then the earth in disarray, the light shines upon it, and God begins to send his apostolic power.

Now I want you to see this as an analogy. The way in which He began everything is how he is going to end everything so that all things will be restored as they were in the beginning. What happened to the earth in Genesis is happening now in the Church.

First God is separating the light from the darkness. This represents the greatest wave of discernment of the spiritual world that is coming upon the body of Christ. The Lord is taking us to levels of light that literally are causing darkness to flee. And this is precisely the "Christ-like Apostles" that was sent to the earth and made flesh.

In the beginning was the Word, and the Word was with God, and the Word was God.

The same was in the beginning with God.

All things were made by him; and without him was not any thing made that was made.

In him was life; and the life was the light of men.

And the light shineth in darkness; and the darkness has not overcome it.

—John 1:1-5

Here we see clearly that when life, which is light, manifests itself, a spiritual war begins that changes the entire atmosphere, dispelling darkness. First we have to delineate Satan's place, throwing him out from among us, so that order, in all things can come into being.

As long as there is darkness inside of us or around us, we will not be able to see the glory of God. And it is the glory that produces the transformation of all things. That is why we must first of all contend with darkness.

For God, who commanded the light to shine out of
darkness, hath shined in our hearts, to give the light
of the knowledge of the glory of God in the face of
Jesus Christ.

—*2 Corinthians 4:6*

The apostolic move is going to bring an extremely high
level of illumination, going beyond the level of salvation.
An astounding clarity is going to come so that the deepest
mysteries of God can be understood.

After light is established and darkness flees to its place,
the Lord is going to separate the waters above from the
waters beneath. What is celestial will be clearly distin-
guished from what is earthly.

Today and throughout past generations, many celestial
things were called earthly, even demonic, total insanity.
And many earthly and human doctrines were called celestial. And this is the confusion of the waters. That is why
they must be separated. This is one of the characteristics of
the apostolic move, bringing revelation and the power of
God, so that we see with clarity what is coming from God
and what is coming from men.

This mixing of the waters allows religious spirits to take
the power from the Church. They have the Church bound
and without liberty to be able to experience the greatness
of celestial things.

When these waters are mixed together, the people are
without direction, and live with masks on, confused, full
of rules and theology, but negating the efficacy of a true
relationship with God.

God is about to bring a radical separation between what comes from Him and what is the result of religion.

He is determined to create an expanse between the two types of waters, and it will become visible, who follows the one type and who follows the other.

Then God said, "Let the waters under the heaven be gathered together unto one place, and let the dry land appear." The position of many things on the earth and in the Church, are overlapped, some on top of others, thereby smothering each other and with their priorities in total chaos. (And this hinders life from being produced.) God could not create anything until the earth was uncovered and the seas were set within their boundaries.

Everything must be in its place for the creative designs of God to be manifested. Likewise, each member of the body of believers must find his position and his calling. Then the waters will fill with life, the earth will produce fruit and the heavens will fill with birds. What that means, is that each ministry in its diversity and in its different function will produce that for which God sent it.

The power of "apostles" (one sent from heaven) will loose over each one of us the activation of our purpose on the earth. When a believer finds himself under a true apostolic authority, he will immediately see how he begins to move toward his calling. He will begin to see himself in a different way. He will begin to see with clarity the qualities that God has given him. He will begin to believe in himself as a Son of God, and his development will be released.

The lack of this anointing produces "bench warmers." That is why it is so important for this revelation and this power to flood the Church of Christ.

First, restoration must come, putting everything into order, and then comes the extraordinary manifestation of the creative power of God. The apostolic power is the divine authority that brings invisible things to the visible realm. The Bible says that everything was made from what was not seen. It was not made from what did not exist. It existed, but not in the material plane.

Creation consisted of transporting things from one realm to another. Every miracle, all riches, each wonder of God was already created in the spiritual world and needed to be transported to the visible plane.

When God unites all things in this dispensation in Jesus Christ, those that are in the heavens as well as those upon the earth, we will see a vast number of miracles and wonders without precedent. And this is another characteristic of the manifestation of the "apostles" of God (what is sent from heaven to earth).

The last part of the creation of Genesis is that God made man in his image and after his likeness. The image of God is Christ seen in man. It is the ability to live in two dimensions at the same time, with all of the supernatural characteristics of Christ. We wrongly think that, because we are human, we are in the image of God. Or because God blew his Spirit into us, we are instantly in the likeness of the Most High. Later in this book, I will dedicate several pages to explaining this in detail.

But what I want to emphasize now is that the apostolic move will raise a generation to the image of God, with literally all of the power and celestial qualities that operate in Jesus: the second Adam, who is the image of the invisible God, the first born of all creation.

The Bible says:

> And God blessed them, and God said unto them, Be fruitful, and multiply, and replenish the earth, and subdue it: and have dominion over the fish of the sea, and over the fowl of the air, and over every living thing that moveth upon the earth.
>
> —*Genesis 1:28*

Man, after the fall, definitely lost the government of this planet, but Jesus came to restore that which was lost. And the sons of God will again have authority. Christ will govern together with his chosen ones.

> And the kingdom and dominion, and the greatness of the kingdom under the whole heaven, shall be given to the people of the saints of the most High, whose kingdom is an everlasting kingdom, and all dominions shall serve and obey him.
>
> —*Daniel 7:27*

God is revealing his government, organizing his chosen ones, in order to reign together with them over all things. This is so we will be able to see, not only churches full of His Glory, but the total transformation of cities and nations, through the light of His knowledge.

2

GOD IS A GOD OF DESIGNS

"All this is in writing," David said, "because the hand of the Lord was upon me, and he gave me under-standing in all the details of the plan."

—*1 Chronicles 28:19*
New International Version

G od is a God of patterns, of order, of designs and wonderfully structured projects. Everything that he made functions in a mathematically perfect and extraordinary manner.

When I look at the universe, I am simply amazed at the exactness with which everything develops. He is most certainly in control of each day, of every night, and He knows every star by name. The cycles of the seasons arrive predictably in the months in which they should.

The entire ecosystem of our planet is perfectly cared for and directed by God. As He himself teaches us, the birds neither sow nor reap, and yet God feeds and protects them. He dresses each spring as if it was going to a party and dresses every winter in purity. Everything is beautiful and perfect in its time.

I have spent whole nights in the jungle, where the hand of man has yet to corrupt anything, where in order to arrive, one must fly over miles and miles of what from the air would appear to be an extensive and impenetrable, green carpet. Inside there is a world of millions of different animal and plant species, that for thousands of years have been reproducing; some dying, others being born, and everything working together for hundred and hundreds of years in perfect order.

I am amazed observing his creation… "Everything was made by Him and for Him." I rejoice in listening to it and in discerning the unspeakable wisdom of God that is present in each structure of the designs. Each created thing from its lowest molecular structure speaks of God and praises God.

Because that which may be known of God is manifest in them; for God hath showed it unto them.

> For the invisible things of him from the creation of the world are clearly seen, being understood by the things that are made…
>
> —*Romans 1:19-20*

God doesn't do anything by chance or for emotional reasons. He does everything according to his models, and God girds himself to the outlines of his designs.

Many times we have failed as the Church, because we want God to submit and respond to the plans of men and the truth is that God only acts according to what He has designed.

In the dawn of the new millennium, God is revealing to us the structures that will bring the greatest manifestation of His glory. These structures will be without a doubt the foundation of the millennial kingdom of the Messiah.

We are living in the most exciting times in the history of mankind. Generation after generation have wanted to see and to live the things that God has prepared for us. Things that eye has not seen and ear has not heard, and has not entered into the heart of man are the things that we are already experiencing. Certainly the glory of the latter house will be greater than the former.

First Design: Who We Are

Understanding who we really are, is the door to the great treasures that God has for us. It is the entrance to the most extraordinary knowledge of the love and power of God. In this small, but great key is established the difference between a victorious life, full of the splendor of God and a life of failure and of limited power.

In order to understand this fully, we must consider a fundamental truth, and this is that man is essentially spirit. Man "does not HAVE a spirit inside of him; man IS SPIRIT." MAN IS A SPIRIT THAT LIVES IN A BODY AND COMMUNICATES AND PERCEIVES THE EXTERIOR WORLD THROUGH HIS SOUL.

In the same way that the natural man can see, hear and perceive the material world, the spirit of man can see, hear and perceive the spiritual world.

When I understand that I am a spirit, I don't have to exert a lot of effort in order to be spiritual, because that is what I am. If, on the contrary, I believe that I am a being of flesh and bone that has a spirit, it will be much harder to believe that I can be spiritual. My mind will make endless conjectures, trying with an incredible force to be spiritual, and will only end up being frustrated. I must understand that it is impossible for a spirit not to be spiritual.

You, dear reader, are spirit, and for that reason you have everything you need in order to be spiritual.

Our spirit came from God. He knows us from before the foundation of the world, because we were in Him and we came from Him.

Before coming to Christ, our spirit is awake to the spiritual world of darkness but dead to God due to sin. When we come to Him through a genuine conversion, by means of a sincere repentance and accepting the sacrifice of the cross, our spirit comes alive again for God.

Now, we are not only spirit, but the Word of God tells us something that changes our whole concept of things:

HE WHO COMES TO JESUS IS JOINED TO THE LORD

1 Corinthians 6:17

Do you see, dear reader, what this means? Take a few minutes and allow these words to penetrate your being... "You are one spirit with Jesus." This means that we are not two separate spirits, He, over there, far away in heaven and me, here, trying to be spiritual. ONE SPIRIT means that He has bonded in such a way with my spirit that I no longer know where He begins and I end and He ends and I begin.

When this revelation becomes the fruit of deep meditation in your life, everything begins to change inside and outside of you. EVERY BORN AGAIN MAN HAS UNITED HIS SPIRIT TO GOD AND FOR THAT REASON IS ABLE TO KNOW GOD INTIMATELY AND HEAR HIS VOICE.

The natural man in us, which is the one that we see and hear with our physical senses, is the one that perceives the natural world, and the spiritual man, which is our spirit, is the one which tunes into the spiritual world.

As the human being matures in his relationship and in his knowledge of God, the spiritual world becomes much more easily perceived. With this I am not referring to a doctrinal knowledge about God, but a vital and continual encounter between the two spirits, God's and yours.

We can spend hours reading the Bible, memorizing hundreds of verses, comparing and basing ourselves upon passages of scripture until we understand a lot about what God is like. And, in spite of all of that effort, we can find ourselves with the fact that we have never had an experience that permits us to know Him face to face, realizing that our spiritual ear is so weak, we practically do not hear the voice of God.

The truth is that we need to spend time with God in the quietness of spirit. We must learn to internalize ourselves in such a way that only the voice of the Spirit is heard. We have to learn to quiet the intense noise of our thoughts, of our mental faculties so full of error, high mindedness, unbelief, fleshliness, and doctrines of men.

I like to spend whole hours just feeling his presence. Sometimes, He allows me to see him openly. Other times we just talk. I have seen unspeakable things in the heavens. He has taken me to chambers of deep mysteries. The spiritual world is Christ revealing himself. "In Him we live, and move, and have our being."

This is the corner stone of the Church, the revelation of Christ in the heart of man, in all of its facets and depth. Jesus asked his disciples:

> He saith unto them, But whom say ye that I am?
>
> And Simon Peter answered and said, Thou art the Christ, the Son of the living God.
>
> And Jesus answered and said unto him, Blessed art thou, Simon Barjona: for flesh and blood hath not revealed it unto thee, but my Father which is in heaven.
>
> And I say also unto thee, That thou art Peter, and upon this rock I will build my church; and the gates of hell shall not prevail against it.
>
> And I will give unto thee the keys of the kingdom of heaven: and whatsoever thou shalt bind on earth shall be bound in heaven: and whatsoever thou shalt loose on earth shall be loosed in heaven.
>
> —*Matthew 16:15-19*

What Jesus is saying, in other words, is the following: "You are Peter. You are like an immovable rock, because of the revelation of Christ in you. Christ, revealed in you in full measure, is what gives you the authority in the heavens and on the earth to govern in the spiritual world and in the natural world. And with the authority that arises from this revelation, the kingdom of darkness will not be able to prevail against you."

Christ wants to reveal himself in our days, as he has never revealed himself to any other generation. God wants to raise up a supernatural Church that knows Him in the depth of His Spirit, a people whose power and authority are the fruit of an intimate and revealed knowledge of Christ in us, the hope of glory.

There is a prophetic mantel of revelation that is falling upon the Church, called to be the bride of the Lamb. Revelation 19:10 says:

> ...The testimony of Jesus is the spirit of prophecy.
> —*Revelation 19:10*

God is bringing a prophetic move without precedent, because He wants to reveal Christ in all of His fullness, so that in that revelation the heavens and the earth operate in one united realm by Christ Jesus.

Second Design: The Union of the Heavens and the Earth

Jesus has a glorious design for these last days and he shows it to us through the Apostle Paul in the book of Ephesians 1:9-10:

> He made known to us the mystery of His will, according to His kind intention which He purposed

in Him with a view to an administration suitable to the fullness of the times, that is, the summing up of all things in Christ, THINGS IN THE HEAVENS AND THINGS UPON THE EARTH.

—*Ephesians 1:9-10*

This means that God has planned not only to reveal the designs and structures of his celestial kingdom, but that heaven manifests in its fullness upon the earth, just like it was in the beginning in the Garden of Eden.

The Bible tells us what Eden was like before the creation of mankind when Lucifer still resided in the heavens.

...Thou sealest up the sum, full of wisdom, and perfect in beauty.

Thou hast been in Eden the garden of God; every precious stone was thy covering...

—*Ezekiel 28:12b, 13a*

When God created man, He put him in the Garden of Eden on the earth. But at that time, nothing separated God from man and nothing divided the heavens and the earth. Adam could see with his natural eyes his spiritual clothing, and could walk with God in the cool of the evening.

This will also be the level of revelation that the glorious Church will experience in the last days.

The testimony of Christ, which is the spirit of prophecy, is one of the most important foundations for what God wants to do in our days (Rev. 19:10).

The testimony of Jesus Christ is eternal. Everything was created by Him and for Him. Everything in the heavens speaks about Him and reveals Him. From the invisible, which is Him, came all matter that makes up the universe. Everything is sustained by His right hand.

The very essence of the prophetic is that Jesus be revealed, that the light of His glory open the eyes of our spirit and we can experience Him, feel Him and see Him just as He is manifest in the heavens. God is unfolding the heavens in a new and extraordinary way, for all those who want to stretch toward a higher and more sublime call, for all those who want to leave behind the old molds of a traditional church and enter into a new move of His Spirit.

It is the birth of an apostolic and prophetic reformation that will take the Church to its maximum potential of power, of triumph, and of revealed knowledge of God, a Church that will, literally, be seated in celestial places with Christ. This will not be a theological position, as we have seen up until now, where people proclaim this position of power, but the reality has been a Church with limited ability to produce any supernatural manifestation of God.

The apostolic and prophetic reformation is a substantial change that God is making in His Church. It is the revelation of Christ as prophet and apostle, bringing the fulfillment of every word He has spoken, bringing the manifestation of the heavens upon the earth. It is the strength of His glorious government over all of creation through His body, which is the Church.

God is choosing in this new reformation those who will govern with Him now and in the millennial reign, and He is already positioning them in a different dimension of spiritual understanding and of communion with Him. Many, around the world, are being caught up into an experience (in the body or outside of the body I do not know), to the third heaven, where God has been training them in an exceptional manner. (In later chapters I will go deeper into this.) I already know more than one hundred who have been there.

God is revealing the spiritual world of darkness in a way we had never before imagined.

> Having made known unto us the mystery of his will, according to his good pleasure which he hath purposed in himself:
>
> That in the dispensation of the fullness of times he might gather together in one all things in Christ, both which are in heaven, and which are on earth.
> —*Ephesians 1:9-10*

The prayer of millions of believers, to whom is being given the understanding of the celestial designs, is causing the designs and the government of God to descend upon the earth.

The believers on earth are releasing power so that the heavens are made to descend. From the heavens God is raising believers and bringing the earth towards Himself.

Between the two realms, the second heaven will be smashed.

The kingdom of darkness is suffering earthquake after earthquake and beneath the earth is also being shaken!

Third Design: The Understanding of the Spiritual World

God reveals to the prophet Daniel the age in which we are living today, the end times:

And at that time shall Michael stand up, the great prince which standeth for the children of thy people: and there shall be a time of trouble, such as never was since there was a nation even to that same time: and at that time thy people shall be delivered, every one that shall be found written in the book.

And many of them that sleep in the dust of the earth shall awake, some to everlasting life, and some to shame and everlasting contempt.

And THEY THAT BE WISE shall shine as the brightness of the firmament; and they that turn many to righteousness as the stars for ever and ever.

—Daniel 12:1-3

These wise men do not refer to those having the message of salvation, but those that understand the designs, the times and the work that God is doing in our days. They are people, who make a difference in the kingdom of darkness, because they shine. They are sons of God who understand spiritual government because they teach righteousness (which, as we will see later, is one of the cornerstones of the foundation of the throne and of the kingdom of God).

Michael, who is the chief of the armies of God, has risen in order to fight in the air the battle that will loose the greatest harvest of all times of "every one that shall be found written in the book." These are the ones who are called to be saved according to the designs of God for their lives, but who are not yet saved because they need to be set free.

In this action led by Michael, we see an indisputable move of spiritual warfare and a number of "they that be wise" who have the illumination and the capacity in the spirit to understand what is happening in the spiritual realm.

Through this passage, the first thing that God wants us to understand is that we move simultaneously in two dimensions that are both linked together—the natural world and the spiritual world. The stronger of the two, is the spiritual world as it is an eternal reality. It is this spiritual world that AFFECTS, TRANSFORMS, MODIFIES, RULES AND STRUCTURES the natural world. What occurs in the spiritual world is going to DETERMINE THE HISTORY of the natural world.

If we want to change the world that surrounds us, transform our communities, affect the thoughts and idiosyncrasies of a nation, it is essential to produce these changes first of all in the spiritual dimension.

The spiritual world is basically and essentially made up of two kingdoms: the Kingdom of Light and the kingdom of darkness. It is the kingdom of darkness that rules as a spiritual government over practically the whole earth.

Ecclesiastes 5:8 says:

If thou seest the oppression of the poor, and violent perverting of judgment and justice in a province, marvel not at the matter: for he that is higher than the highest regardeth; and there be higher than they.

—*Ecclesiastes 5:8*

Here you can see clearly how a structure of hierarchies of oppression affects the natural world.

God allowed the Apostle Paul to understand the spiritual world, to look into it and to reveal it to us in his epistles. I believe, and this is only my opinion, that when he was caught up to the third heaven, he saw the designs of God, and he was permitted to see from above all of the organizational structure of the kingdom of darkness. I believe this because of the way in which he tries to communicate to the Ephesians about the different levels of the demonic powers in the heavenly regions. He talks about principalities, of powers, and of rulers of darkness, of hosts of wickedness, and these are not synonymous with the word demons, but are a clearly understood structure of the kingdom of darkness. In the epistle to the Colossians, he adds another two hierarchies that are over the ones previously mentioned, which are thrones and dominions.

Paul talks to us about these things due to their obvious importance in understanding the spiritual world.

One thing that is undeniably true; the more we know about the spiritual world, the easier it will be for us to apply the principles of the kingdom of Light, which will drive out the kingdom of darkness.

The purpose of these lines, therefore, is to help you to understand the plans and designs of God, as well as the designs of the devil, in order to take the Church to the total victory that Christ won for her on the cross of Calvary.

Spiritual Cities

God reveals the spiritual world to us through his word, through types, symbols, parables, and analogies, together with historical events and through clear descriptions of his kingdom revealed to the prophets, and undeniable visitations by celestial messengers.

One teaching that we have learned and that God has revealed to Dr. Morris Cerullo is that ALL TRUTH IS PARALLEL. Based on this, we can observe how societies throughout the centuries have built cities in order to establish themselves. Cities are seats of government. It is in the major cities of a nation where the social organizations are found that determine the history and the development of each country. It is in the cities, where the main religious temples, as well as the financial institutions that sustain the population, are established. For this reason, when we talk about government and structure, the concept of city is one of the most important concepts that we can study.

The book of Revelation reveals to us this type of structure of darkness in chapter 17, verse 18:

> And the woman which thou sawest is that great city, which reigneth over the kings of the earth.
> —*Revelation 17:18*

For many reasons, we can know that this does not refer to a specific city on the face of the earth, but rather to a structure of demonic government, symbolized by the image of a city.

The word says that this structure of darkness is reigning at the present time, since it does not refer to something that is going to become manifest in the future. This woman is also called Babylon the great. We know that the Babylonian principles of confusion, as its name suggests (Babel means confusion), operate in every nation through false religions, philosophies or dictators that separate man from

God. It has been this way since the times of the Tower of Babel until our days.

Then a formation or spiritual structure exists in the celestial regions from which the different demonic governments on the face of the earth depend. There not only exists a city of darkness that governs the nations, but also a celestial city and a divine structure, which are the ones that God wants to establish upon the earth. And it is this divine structure or design that we want to discuss as we go along in this book.

Ezekiel, who saw the glory of God and who was immersed innumerable times in the designs of God, was transported in the spirit in order to see this grand structure in the heavens.

> In the visions of God brought he me into the land of Israel, and set me upon a very high mountain, by which was as the frame of a city on the south...
>
> And the man said unto me, Son of man, behold with thine eyes, and hear with thine ears, and set thine heart upon all that I shall show thee; for to the intent that I might show them unto thee art thou brought hither: declare all that thou seest to the house of Israel.
>
> —*Ezekiel 40:2 and 4*

God tells him to see, to listen to and to set his heart upon the vision. And this is an essential key for the great depths of the kingdom of the heavens to be revealed to us.

The prophet Daniel, to whom God opened the spiritual world so he could see one of the most extraordinary angelic battles, said:

Yea, while I was speaking in prayer, even the man Gabriel, whom I had seen in the vision at the beginning, being caused to fly swiftly, touched me about the time of the evening oblation.

And he informed me, and talked with me, and said, O Daniel, I am now come forth to give thee skill and understanding.

At the beginning of thy supplications the commandment came forth, and I am come to show thee; for thou art greatly beloved: therefore understand the matter, and consider the vision.

—Daniel 9:21-23

The great prophetic move that God released upon Daniel for the liberation of Israel was loosed upon a man who regretted, understanding the structure and designs that would bring the people back to God and would release them from captivity. He prayed, and begged, and confessed the sin of his people. He did not stop until he had literally shaken the structures of the government in the second heaven. His prayer activated Gabriel, and the understanding to mobilize the heavens was given to him.

I can tell you, dear reader, without any fear of being mistaken, that that same Gabriel is being mobilized by God to bring the revelation and the understanding that will establish, according to the designs of God, the great celestial city and the government of God upon the earth. God is sending his army of angels upon every nation, so that, together with the Church, they can carry out His designs.

Are they not all ministering spirits, sent forth to
minister for them who shall be heirs of salvation?
—*Hebrews 1:14*

The angel that spoke with Ezekiel in the great revelation of the celestial city said to him:

And if they be ashamed of all that they have done,
show them the design of the house...
—*Ezekiel 43:11*

A glorious move of prayer, of crying out and a sincere
thirst to seek God has been loosed upon the whole earth.
Revelation is coming upon the face of the earth as never
before, and a powerful awakening of the prophetic and
apostolic anointing are descending from on high.

Fourth Design: The Kingdom of God Will Govern the Earth

When we talk about kingdoms, kingdoms of light as well
as of darkness, we are referring to systems of government. A
kingdom exists with the purpose of ruling through a structure of power, of thought, of behavior, of laws, of economy,
etc., and it submits under its regime all of its subjects.

On earth every government is recognized by the inhabitants of their countries, and the people submit themselves
to their respective kings or presidents.

The Kingdom of the heavens is about to manifest itself in
a surprising manner. The design of God is to govern, and
Jesus is preparing His millennial kingdom and choosing
those who will govern with Him.

(The mission of the different ministries of Jesus Christ is to establish the Kingdom of God upon the face of the planet, and for this to occur, we need to understand how the Kingdom works.)

Our battle then, is how to eradicate the government of the devil and how to establish the government of God. It is then a war, not between isolated beings, each one fighting for his little piece of ground, as if we were all desert nomads; but it is a fierce battle in the spiritual world that will oust one government in order to establish another.

Until now, we as individuals have gotten used to some of the principles of the kingdom of God being established in our own lives and in some members of our communities. Nevertheless, the will of God for our times goes much further than that. The heart of God wants to govern over entire nations and over the whole earth. God is not satisfied with a small remnant of apparently faithful people, who in the background are fighting and criticizing one another.

God wants to reign over every nation. His final design is that the heavens and the earth be united in Christ Jesus. He is King in the heavens and He wants to be the effective and true King over all the earth.

Isn't our daily prayer, "Your will be done, on earth as it is in heaven," "Your kingdom come?"

We can't bring the kingdom of heaven upon us without understanding what kingdom and government are.

When I refer to spiritual government, I am not referring to the governmental order of the local church, nor to a system of hierarchy that controls the people of God; but to something higher, to the sublime government of the heavens over the nations of the earth and over every created thing.

Jesus gave us through his victory on the cross all power against the kingdom of darkness:

Behold, I give unto you power to tread on serpents and scorpions, and over all the power of the enemy: and nothing shall by any means hurt you.

—*Luke 10:19*

Authority has to do with principles of the Kingdom of God. The vast majority of Christians do not have the least bit of authority, because they live in an independent, unstructured and errant manner. And I am not only talking about Christians who are church members, but to entire churches that are similar to small tribes, disconnected from any union with the Kingdom.

The sad thing is, Satan and his people understand spiritual principles with much more clarity than the average Christian does. Satan knows that every spiritual law originates in God, and what he does is to take these principles, pervert them and make them work. And in this way, he surpasses us in many ways.

I am reminded of a story of diverse people who lived dispersed, like the nomadic groups of the deserts of Africa and Arabia. They didn't have power or authority until a man, with "kingdom vision," united them under the great empire, known today as the Islamic nations. Mohammed, their leader, prophet as they call him, understood that in order to govern and to establish the violent and cruel principles of Islam, he had to unite the dispersed tribes. Today, the fight to liberate millions of Muslims from slavery is a fierce battle against a strongly organized government in the second heaven.

What God wants us to understand is that the authority that He gave us is not just to liberate those possessed with demons and to heal the sick, but it has to do with governing with Christ Jesus.

In the natural realm, the strength of a country resides in the unity and the solidarity of its inhabitants, in their commitment and national consciousness. It resides in the confidence they have in those who govern them and in the conviction to give their lives for the ideals of their country. It depends upon the power of their armies and the strength of their international bonds. It rests in the economic stability and the financial aspirations of its inhabitants. And all of this makes the nation grow and prosper. But, above everything else, it depends on who their god is.

> Blessed is the nation whose God is the LORD; and the people whom he hath chosen for his own inheritance.
>
> —*Psalms 33:12*

We see this same pattern in the designs of God for the end times. Let's consider Israel, who is the pattern in the natural of what God wants to do in the spiritual with the Church. During the whole time of the dispersion of the Jews, God's people in the flesh were an isolated people, gathered in small communities. They were a people united by the principles of God and by their blood bonds, but they were not a nation. They had no power upon the earth, or opinion, or rights. They were a people without a government, and any nation who want to persecute them, kill them, humiliate them, and rob them, simply did it.

The time came when God gathered them from the confines of the earth. It didn't matter if they were legalistic or orthodox or simple in their faith. Forgotten, strangers, and foreigners among the nations, God began to visit them. Their hearts began to move towards just one direction: To be an established nation, a nation recognized by the earth and inhabiting the land that God at one time had given them!

An anointing of unity, of faith and of government fell upon millions of Jews, and in 1948 the decree was signed: "Israel was now a nation." THE DESIGNS OF GOD WERE FULFILLED UPON THE EARTH.

The same thing is happening with the Church of Jesus Christ, the spiritual Israel. The design of God is not for there to be a bunch of small churches or isolated and dispersed denominations in the middle of nations that are governed by demonic principles, and just like Israel, are humiliated, persecuted and killed.

The design of God is a spiritual Nation that governs over all of the kingdoms of the earth.

> But ye are a chosen generation, a royal priesthood, A
> HOLY NATION, a peculiar people…
>
> —*1 Peter 2:9*

And it also says about His governing people, symbolized by Mount Zion:

> And it shall come to pass IN THE LAST DAYS, that
> the mountain of the Lord's house shall be established

in the top of the mountains, and shall be exalted above the hills; and all nations shall flow unto it.

—*Isaiah 2:2*

Mountains are symbols of government, of established kingdoms, and they are set on high in order to rule everything that is below them.

By faith Abraham, when he was called to go out into a place which he should after receive for an inheritance, obeyed; and he went out, not knowing whither he went.

By faith he sojourned in the land of promise, as in a strange country, dwelling in tabernacles with Isaac and Jacob, the heirs with him of the same promise:

For he looked for A CITY WHICH HATH FOUNDATIONS, WHOSE BUILDER AND MAKER IS GOD.

—*Hebrews 11:8-10*

God wants us to no longer be people beaten down and subjugated by the pharaohs of our days. He wants us to become the city full of the power of God that entered in to posses the land in the times of Joshua. He wants us to be the nation that the devil and all of our enemies fear, because the glory of the Lord of hosts is seen upon us.

Arise, shine; for thy light is come, and the glory of the LORD is risen upon thee.

For, behold, the darkness shall cover the earth, and gross darkness the people: but the LORD shall arise upon thee, and HIS GLORY SHALL BE SEEN UPON THEE.

AND THE GENTILES SHALL COME TO THY LIGHT, AND KINGS TO THE BRIGHTNESS OF THY RISING.

—Isaiah 60:1-3

His glory will be visible and the Church, the nation of God will govern over all the kingdoms of the earth.

Ever since I came to the feet of Jesus Christ, I have known that it is the Church of our Lord that has the power over every kind of evil, and over any type of organization of darkness. Through the ministry of warfare, I have confronted several of perhaps the strongest powers of the devil upon the earth. And, on various occasions, God has allowed me to come face to face with Satan.

I have seen innumerable victories over the empire of evil in almost every one of its forms, not only in my ministry, but also in other powerful ministries of warfare and liberation upon the earth. That is why I know, from experience, that there is no power greater in the universe than that of Jesus Christ and the power He grants to his servants.

Nevertheless, although God is in control over the whole earth, and nothing happens without His will, we see that the principles of God are not the governing entity over the nations. As it says in the book of Hebrews:

Thou hast put all things in subjection under his feet. For in that he put all in subjection under him, he left nothing that is not put under him. BUT NOW WE SEE NOT YET ALL THINGS PUT UNDER HIM.

—Hebrews 2:8

It also says:

But this man, after he had offered one sacrifice for sins for ever, sat down on the right hand of God;

From henceforth expecting till his enemies be made his footstool.

—*Hebrews 10:12 and 13*

When He says that He is waiting until "they are made," this clearly means that someone else will do it, and that someone is the Church.

Returning to what pulses through my veins, which is that the authority of Jesus is above all other authority, something happened to me that changed my whole perspective in seeing things.

God began to awaken in me a vision that made me shake with horror. I saw the crushing strength of the kingdom of darkness, whose armies were organized, its generals coordinated, and its support fronts distributed throughout the whole earth. All of them fought for the same cause. Their principalities and governors were united and perfectly structured, in order to carry out Satan's plans in the highest political, economic, and religious spheres upon the face of the planet.

Impressive hierarchies of darkness were positioned under the guise of secret societies. They not only governed in the visible realms of earthly governments, but their diabolical plans were protected through underground powers that were undetectable on the surface and therefore almost indestructible.

There were supply lines that strengthened it from all parts of the world. Millions of demons went forth throughout the world inciting people to sin and to shed blood. This caused the walls of their fortresses to become stronger and insurmountable.

The kingdom of darkness had under its control the riches of the powerful of the earth. I saw their armies obey when they were sent to destroy churches and to finish off the ministers of God. The ones most attacked were the ones that were alone. I saw the demons entering the churches, and there was practically no opposition when spirits were sent in of pride and self-sufficiency, of gossip and division, of sex and greed and of power.

I saw the Church as little lights dispersed in the nations, wanting to fight against the organized and terribly hideous government.

While my heart felt remorse with the vision, God confronted my soul and said to me, "Don't let your heart faint at the vision, because the time has come in which I will descend in order to govern the earth. The heavens and the earth will be one in this dispensation. I am choosing those who will govern at my side."

While He talked with me, like a lightening bolt the scripture came to my spirit that says:

> These shall make war with the Lamb, and the Lamb shall overcome them: for he is Lord of lords, and King of kings: and they that are with him are called, and chosen, and faithful.
>
> —*Revelation 17:14*

The question that inevitably arises is how to do it? How is the kingdom of darkness structured? How can we bring the conflict to light in order to win? What are the glorious revelations of the Kingdom of God that will give us the total victory?

God is opening the Book of the end times. And the entrance to possessing the Kingdom of God is before us. The purpose of these pages is the revelation that God gave me of the things that are about to happen, so that Christ will return and govern upon the earth.

3

THE CONFLICT REALITY OF THE TWO KINGDOMS

In order to reach a deep understanding that will produce victory over the government of evil, we must understand how the spiritual world works, what its laws are, and how to become truly influential beings in this invisible world.

The true conflict is a confrontation between light and darkness. As the Apostle John says:

> In him was life; and the life was the light of men. And the light shineth in darkness; and the darkness comprehended it not.
>
> —*John 1:4-5*

One principle is: Darkness becomes inane in the light. I don't have to shout at the darkness for three hours every time I turn on a light in my house. The darkness automatically disappears, upon the instantaneous manifestation of the light,.

Now if Jesus is the light that abides in us, why doesn't the darkness around us disappear immediately?

The answer is that a large portion of the light is still veiled due to real, substantial structures that the devil has built through men. These veils of darkness produce the same effect as if a light bulb were to be surrounded by a solid shell. The light exists. It is real. It dwells in the believers, but it is veiled by the forces of evil.

Then, one thing is the presence of the light in the lives of those who have been made sons of God, and, another thing, is its visible manifestation through the lives of the believers.

There is an important difference between the presence of the divine virtues and their open manifestation in us. By faith, a new convert has within him the presence of all of the attributes and power of God. Nevertheless, they are not manifest in an immediate manner. The breaking down of the inner man and understanding the principles that produce the manifestation of the light and of the kingdom of God are needed. Then, these attributes and the power of God will be visible to the eyes of others.

What, then, are these veils and structures, and how have they been placed upon us and upon our nations?

And he will destroy in this mountain the face of the covering cast over all people, and the veil that is spread over all nations.

—Isaiah 25:7

In later chapters, we will see different levels of light in the kingdom of God and how to progress in these levels.

The Great Shell:
The Structure Of Iniquity

Ever since the beginning, when the Archangel Lucifer corrupted his holiness and fell from the kingdom of God, the word says:

> You were blameless in your ways from the day you were created till wickedness was found in you.
> —*Ezekiel 28:15 NIV*

And later it says:

> Thou hast defiled thy sanctuaries by the multitude of thine iniquities, by the iniquity of thy traffic...
> —*Ezekiel 28:18*

These two words, wickedness and iniquity, that many times are used so casually, are key in being able to understand the configuration of our enemy's empire.

Wickedness arises from the heart and is comprised of the sum total of the thoughts or intentions of the inner man that are opposed to righteousness, goodness, and everything that God is. Wickedness is the origin that will give substance to lust. It is the seed that is going to be sown in the heart of man and is going to be an ever-present root of perverse desires. As the epistle of James says:

> But every man is tempted, when he is drawn away of his own lust, and enticed.

> Then when lust hath conceived, it bringeth forth sin:
> and sin, when it is finished, bringeth forth death.
>
> —*James 1:14-15*

At the time of his fall, man ate of the fruit of wickedness, and, ever since, the direction and the designs of God upon the life of Adam began to move off track, and the straight path became crooked, and it is then that we see iniquity come forth.

Iniquity means etymologically "that which is twisted." Therefore, it is the accumulated total of wickedness that is twisting man's walk. It is like the spiritual genetic cord, in which the sins of man are recorded, and that which will determine what is to be inherited by the next generation. It is where the twisted, sinful legacy is engraved that a man will leave for his children. These children will in turn twist the legacy even more with their own sins, and they will pass the baton of wickedness to the subsequent generation.

> The sin of Judah is written with a pen of iron, and
> with the point of a diamond: it is graven upon the
> table of their heart...
>
> —*Jeremiah 17:1*

Iniquity is, therefore, one of the most important words mentioned in the Bible. It is also one of the most misunderstood and least preached subjects. It is through iniquity that the devil is going to obtain material in order to build entire cities and structures of evil.

It is in that recorded area in our spirit where the sin data of our generations is stored. It is right there that wickedness, coming from our ancestors, is linked together. It is in this same area where the legal basis of infirmities takes root and is transferred from parents to children, to grandchildren, and so on.

God himself said:

> … For I the LORD thy God am a jealous God, visiting the iniquity of the fathers upon the children unto the third and fourth generation of them that hate me;
>
> —*Exodus 20:5*

The vast majority of believers confess their sins to God, but they have never asked Him to erase their iniquities. And they continue suffering the consequences of terrible financial curses, or sickness, or the destruction of their families, accidents and tragedies, without understanding why this is happening to them. One thing are the sinful acts that we have committed, and, another thing, is the sum total of our wickedness and that of our forefathers that has been engraved inside of us.

David called out to God, saying:

> …Have mercy upon me, O God, according to thy loving kindness: according unto the multitude of thy tender mercies blot out my transgressions.
>
> Wash me thoroughly from mine iniquity, and cleanse me from my sin.
>
> Behold, I was shapen in iniquity, and in sin did my mother conceive me.
>
> —*Psalm 51:1, 2 and 5*

Notice how he deals not only with sin, the acts committed against God, but also with the root and origin that led him to sin.

When the glory of God was made manifest to Moses, the Lord himself said:

> ... The LORD, The LORD God, merciful and gracious, long-suffering, and abundant in goodness and truth,
>
> Keeping mercy for thousands, forgiving iniquity and transgression and sin, and that will by no means clear the guilty...
>
> —*Exodus 34:6b and 7a*

We are going to take a deeper look at the consequences of iniquity, but I want you to begin assimilating this from a point of view less individual and more corporal, since what interests us in this book is being able to perceive the government of evil upon the nations.

What is true for an individual is also true for the group of individuals that make up a society.

The prophet Habakkuk said:

> Woe to him that buildeth a town with blood, and ESTABLISHETH A CITY BY INIQUITY!
>
> —*Habakkuk 2:12*

Obviously it refers here to a spiritual city.

Just as human lives, their actions, and their wickedness are intertwined, iniquity can be said to sew a net. As it goes along, it becomes a thick fortress, capturing its prisoners along the way. It is then that we hear of cases, even among Christians, who sincerely are in a pit, from which they cannot escape.

He made a pit, and digged it, and is fallen into the
ditch which he made.

His mischief shall return upon his own head, and his
violent dealing shall come down upon his own pate.
—*Psalm 7:15-16*

In the same way as with an individual, iniquity also
continues binding and burying nations more and more.
Whole cities are swallowed in spiritual pits of captivity due
to iniquity.

The heathen are sunk down in the pit that they made:
in the net which they hid is their own foot taken.

... The wicked is snared in the work of his own
hands.
—*Psalm 9:15 and 16b*

Iniquity is rooted in the spirit of man, but it is manifest
in the natural world through sickness, curses, shame, and
injustice. In an individual, the affected part is the body, as
well as the attraction of negative circumstances by the spiritual world that is contaminated. The individual is going to
continually suffer damage to his honor and calamities will
occur around him. Let us remember that it is the spiritual
world that dictates to and rules the natural world.

In a nation, the ground becomes infertile and the climate,
in the natural as well as in the social environment, becomes
hostile, oppressive, and even deadly. There is a flow of
violence, drought, hurricanes, terrible floods, and fires as a
consequence of the roots of iniquity.

Physically, iniquity manifests itself with all kinds of sicknesses, such as cancer, diabetes and other illnesses of a hereditary variety.

> As he clothed himself with cursing like as with his garment, so let it come into his bowels like water, and like oil into his bones.
>
> —*Psalm 109:18*

All of the foundation of mankind, as well as that of his cities, is impregnated with curse. It is like a literal substance that attracts to itself every type of evil. Everything that man does and the way in which he develops affects the earth.

> ... Do ye indeed speak righteousness, O congregation? Do ye judge uprightly, O ye sons of men?
>
> Yea, in heart ye work wickedness; YE WEIGH THE VIOLENCE OF YOUR HANDS IN THE EARTH.
>
> —*Psalm 58:1-2*

Iniquity affects the spiritual ear of the believer, as well as the unbeliever, even from birth. And this is the reason why so many have difficulty hearing the voice of God.

> The wicked are estranged from the womb: they go astray as soon as they be born, speaking lies.
>
> Their poison is like the poison of a serpent: they are like the deaf adder that stoppeth her ear;
>
> —*Psalm 58:3-4*

As long and the believer has not confessed his iniquity, it continues affecting him, not his salvation, because he is justified before God with the blood of Jesus, but it does affect his spiritual walk upon the earth. The offence, that means an attack on the honor of the person, and the injustice committed to his ancestors will come upon his life with no apparent reason, as well as curses of every type.

There is a lot of teaching today about the canceling of curses, but I have seen this fail time after time, because iniquity was never dealt with, which is where the curse is rooted. The answer is to recognize it and confess it.

> If they shall confess their iniquity, and the iniquity of their fathers, with their trespass which they trespassed against me, and that also they have walked contrary unto me;
>
> And that I also have walked contrary unto them, and have brought them into the land of their enemies; if then their uncircumcised hearts be humbled, and they then accept of the punishment of their iniquity:
>
> Then will I remember my covenant with Jacob, and also my covenant with Isaac, and also my covenant with Abraham will I remember; AND I WILL REMEMBER THE LAND.
>
> —*Leviticus 26:40-42*

If, under a spirit of honesty, we can analyze and make a healthy critique, and cry out about the condition of our own lives, that of our church, and of our nations, we are going to loose the greatest revival in history and walk towards the true government of God.

If we have the nerve to see what is wrong in ourselves and we have the courage to change it, we will have victory over darkness.

Isn't it iniquity that divides us as brothers, that which makes us judge, without a cause, those who we have not even spoken to, and gotten to know, or at least listened to? Perhaps we are immersed in a system full of religiosity, of prominent masks, of created interests, of jealousy, envy, and gossip?

We see people drug around by the devil every day, robbed workers, beaten up servants, due to horrible circumstances. We see brothers die. We see violent sicknesses destroy those we love. We see the destruction of homes by aberrant sins, and, so many times, it seems that there is no answer. We preach the power of the resurrection and the light of the truth, while millions of believers live in defeat, hidden behind masks of lies. They spend their lives hiding sin, disguised in Sunday-morning holiness, with lives full of deceit, bound by the desires of the flesh that they no longer even attempt to conquer.

We seek numbers and even greater numbers in our churches. We drink the balm of the lie, "10,000 were saved in the crusade!" And that shuts up the deafening sound of the uncommitted Church, without love, a Church entertained with eloquent sermons that has no knowledge of the power of the true light and of the true conversion.

In no way do I want to generalize, but it is my desire that together we can drive the hatchet into the root of the problem, and be able to bring the bountiful light of God upon our nations.

The truth is that the structure of the heavenly government does not rule our nations. Nevertheless, Jesus wants to do it, but he must shake us first.

We cry out and we groan for the salvation of our nations, but it is time to listen to what He wants to say.

> Behold, the LORD'S hand is not shortened, that it cannot save; neither his ear heavy, that it cannot hear:
>
> But your iniquities have separated between you and your God, and your sins have hid his face from you, that he will not hear.
>
> For your hands are defiled with blood, and your fingers with iniquity; your lips have spoken lies, your tongue hath muttered perverseness.
>
> None calleth for justice, nor any pleadeth for truth: they trust in vanity, and speak lies; they conceive mischief, and bring forth iniquity.
>
> —*Isaiah 59:1-4*

And it continues in verse 9:

> Therefore is judgment far from us, neither doth justice overtake us: we wait for light, but behold obscurity; for brightness, but we walk in darkness.
>
> —*Isaiah 59:9*

The truth is that if we do not do something radical, for us, for the Church, and for our nation, we will not have the strength to confront and to rescue a world immersed in the darkest levels of darkness, as is this generation of the new millennium.

4

PRINCIPLES OF THE KINGDOM: THE THRONE OF GOD

I beheld till the thrones were cast down, and the Ancient of days did sit, whose garment was white as snow, and the hair of his head like the pure wool: his throne was like the fiery flame, and his wheels as burning fire.

A fiery stream issued and came forth from before him: thousand thousands ministered unto him, and ten thousand times ten thousand stood before him: the judgment was set, and the books were opened.

—Daniel 7:9-10

I saw in the night visions, and, behold, one like the Son of man came with the clouds of heaven, and

came to the Ancient of days, and they brought him
near before him.

And there was given him dominion, and glory, and
a kingdom, that all people, nations, and languages,
should serve him: his dominion is an everlasting
dominion, which shall not pass away, and his kingdom
that which shall not be destroyed.

—*Daniel 7:13-14*

The kingdom of heaven is established around the great
throne of God. In this kingdom all truth is perfect,
absolute, and immovable. It is this divine design, the
one that Jesus Christ will establish upon the earth, and His
saints will govern with Him.

We know that, after the apocalyptic events, a millennial
kingdom will come, in which Christ will reign for 1,000
years and that the devil will be bound during this time.
(Revelation 20:1-3) Nevertheless, the government of Jesus
will begin to manifest itself and to prepare itself before this
occurs in its final form. God is equipping those who will sit
in order to judge together with Him.

And I saw thrones, and they sat upon them, and
judgment was given unto them…

—*Revelation 20:4a*

He has purposed that a magnificent Church be seen by
every nation, upon which His own glory will shine. The
kings of the earth will walk in her light, and the riches of
the nations will be given to her. (Isaiah 60, paraphrased)

Jesus is preparing a bride who is holy, without spot or wrinkle. This will be the condition of His beloved before He comes for her.

He is training a warrior Church that will bring to the feet of Jesus the greatest harvest of souls of all times.

> ... And at that time thy people shall be delivered, EVERY ONE that shall be found written in the book.
>
> *—Daniel 12:1b*

Those who are wise, as Daniel calls them, will act and exert themselves. And it will be clear in their eyes what God wants to do at this time of destiny for humanity.

Previously, we spoke about the difference between the presence of a divine virtue and God's open manifestation among men. Let us see, from this point of view, the most important part of the kingdom of heaven: the throne of God.

> The LORD reigneth; let the earth rejoice; let the multitude of isles be glad thereof.

> Clouds and darkness are round about him: RIGHTEOUSNESS AND JUDGMENT ARE THE HABITATION OF HIS THRONE.

> A FIRE goeth before him, and burneth up his enemies round about.

> His lightnings enlightened the world: the earth saw, and trembled.

The hills melted like wax at the presence of the
LORD, at the presence of the Lord of the whole
earth.

The heavens DECLARE HIS RIGHTEOUSNESS,
AND ALL THE PEOPLE SEE HIS GLORY.
—*Psalm 97:1-6*

The cry of every believer is that the government of God
be visible upon every nation. We pray for His kingdom to
come among mankind. For this to happen, the first thing
that will descend upon the earth is the manifestation of his
throne.

Righteousness and judgment are the foundation of his
throne. And these two principles are inseparable and operate
in harmony with the designs of God, in order to bring his
glory upon the earth. When these two foundations descend
upon a place, the enemies of God are put under the soles of
His feet, and the glorious manifestation of His presence is
felt, bringing His will among us.

Righteousness is one of the attributes of God himself.
God is just. Righteousness is latent upon our lives, and,
although we are justified and declared righteous before God
by His grace, we do not enjoy the benefits of righteousness until God establishes it upon our lives. As opposed
to iniquity, in which is engraved unrighteousness, curse,
offence, calamity, sickness, etc., when righteousness is established upon our lives, all of the benefits of the kingdom of
God come upon us.

That is why many believers read the impressive promises
of God upon the righteous, but the truth is that there are

few that enjoy their fullness. The reason is that positionally they are made righteous before God, but righteousness has not yet been established upon them here on the earth.

When I speak of establishing, I mean something that is founded in an immovable way upon a life; when it is made visible in the earthly realm; when a celestial truth is made evident in a person or in a people.

Jesus said we were not to be worried or anxious about anything, not about what were to eat, or for what we were to drink, or wear. All of these things are going to be added to us if we seek first the kingdom of God and its righteousness.

What Jesus is saying is that when the throne of God is truly founded and established in the heart of man, everything that pertains to the kingdom of heaven is attracted towards that throne.

Now, the conflict is that, just as love cannot stop loving, righteousness will inevitably judge. The purpose of righteousness is to align all things to the designs of God. On the one hand, it establishes the kingdom of God and His government upon the earth, and, on the other hand, sentences that which opposes Him.

The problem with which we find ourselves is the word "judgment." We prefer to erase it from our Bibles. Due to fear, or for religious reasons, such an enormous misunderstanding has been created about this word that we avoid it at all cost.

One of the greatest offenses that someone can give a Christian in tribulation, is to say to them: "This is the judgment of God upon your life." We look for all of the super-spiritual reasons in order to justify what is going on in our lives. Anything is better, than to accept the word "judgment."

We have converted it into a horrible word that catalogues the Christian in question as "bad," or "undesirable," as one who has left "the perfect holiness" in which the entire church, without exception, walks (as many ironically believe). Now he is singled out by the destructive wrath of God. And then, we need to be careful of that Christian, since he, most surely, must have something hidden that was what attracted this terrible "judgment" to him.

Nothing is more incorrect and less understood than the paragraph you have just read. The judgment of God is a divine foundation and, since it is part of the very foundation of His throne, it has to do with the main designs of the government of the kingdom of God.

God is good and everything that is, and everything that surrounds His throne, is sublime and wonderful. There is nothing horrible in heaven and much less in the foundation of His government.

Therefore, I am asking you to set aside any previous concept you may have had about this word, and open your spirit to something glorious that God wants to do in our lives.

Let's imagine a scene that illustrates what is happening in the spiritual world. You receive official notification that you have inherited a multi-million dollar ranch. The problem is that it is located in an area in which the testator had many enemies, who do not want you to be the new owner of the ranch. You get up your courage and go there to claim what is now your inheritance.

The ranch is occupied by innumerable roughnecks, who have begun to ransack the house, and, from the first moment you arrive, they grab you among several of them. They tie your hands and feet, and they say to you, "These ropes are because of what your parents did." Then they begin to poke you and to hurt your body. And another one shouts, "This is for what your grandfather did." Another one arrives, takes all of your belongings, and begins to yell, "This is because you deserve it, due to your own wickedness."

Then, you, who are angry and indignant about what they are doing, start shouting at them that you are the owner of the property and that you have the authority to throw them out and put them into jail for what they have done. They look at you, tied up on the floor, and laugh at you, while the leader of the group sits in the landowner's chair and destroys the ranch at his whim.

You begin to feel the oppression of the offence and of the injustice, of the plunder, and of the terrible evil that has been done to you, when you innocently decided to claim your inheritance. You are the true owner. All of the riches of the ranch are yours, together with all of the future earnings. But you can't enjoy it because the injustice, and your own sin have bound you and will not permit you to manifest the power that you rightly possess.

The only way that you will obtain victory, is if your case goes to court. UNTIL THE COURT DECIDES IN YOUR FAVOR, JUSTICE CANNOT DEFEND YOU.

ALL JUDGMENT HAS A WINNER AND A LOSER, AND THE GOOD NEWS IS THAT IN CHRIST JESUS WE ARE MORE THAN CONQUERORS. AND IT

IS TIME FOR THE DEFEAT OF THE DEVIL TO BE
SEEN IN ITS ENTIRE SPLENDOR.

David said in Psalm 7:

> Arise, O LORD, in thine anger, lift up thyself because
> of the rage of mine enemies: and awake for me to the
> judgment that thou hast commanded.
>
> So shall the congregation of the people compass thee
> about: for their sakes therefore return thou on high.
>
> The LORD shall judge the people: judge me, O
> LORD, according to my righteousness, and according
> to mine integrity that is in me.
>
> Oh let the wickedness of the wicked come to an end;
> but ESTABLISH THE JUST...
>
> —*Psalm 7:6-9*

We have, as our inheritance, all things that pertain to
the kingdom of heaven, but we do not enter into possession
of them until righteousness is established upon us, through
the Supreme Court that executes God's justice.

David fully understood the meaning of this word. He
said again:

> ... The judgments of the LORD are true and righteous
> altogether.
>
> MORE TO BE DESIRED ARE THEY THAN
> GOLD, yea, than much fine gold: SWEETER also
> than honey and the honeycomb.
>
> —*Psalm 19:9b-10*

How can we talk about desirable and sweet judgment? The earth, as we saw previously, is covered by strongholds of iniquity. And this iniquity has been rooted for generations upon all human beings, including Christians. Judgment has to do directly with iniquity. God is sending a judgment of wrath against the iniquity that governs this world, and he is loosing a judgment of mercy upon those who seek his kingdom and his righteousness. This is in order to cleanse us from the spiritual dross that impedes all of the blessings of God from being loosed upon us.

Judgment is sweet when it brings a revelation of those areas of our heart (that we don't even know exist) that the devil is using to rob us of the bounty of God.

There is no greater virtue in a man than the humility to recognize is own iniquity. David said:

Wash me thoroughly from mine iniquity, and cleanse me from my sin.

For I acknowledge my transgressions: and my sin is ever before me.

Against thee, thee only, have I sinned, and done this evil in thy sight: THAT THOU MIGHTEST BE JUSTIFIED WHEN THOU SPEAKEST, AND BE CLEAR WHEN THOU JUDGEST.

—*Psalm 51:2-4*

Jesus said:

Blessed are they which do hunger and thirst after righteousness: for they shall be filled.

—*Matthew 5:6*

God wants to bring His kingdom upon us in all the splendor of His glory, but He needs to root out iniquity in order to establish his throne.

The times in which God would descend in order to establish His kingdom and how He would act among His people were revealed to the Prophet Malachi.

Behold, I will send my messenger, and he shall prepare the way before me: and the Lord, whom ye seek, shall suddenly come to his temple, even the messenger of the covenant, whom ye delight in: behold, he shall come, saith the LORD of hosts.

But who may abide the day of his coming? And who shall stand when he appeareth? For he is like a refiner's fire, and like fullers' soap:

And he shall sit as a refiner and purifier of silver: and he shall purify the sons of Levi, and purge them as gold and silver, that they may offer unto the LORD an offering IN RIGHTEOUSNESS.

—Malachi 3:1-3

Let us note in this passage that God is showing us a visitation of Jesus Christ that is not the rapture or the Second Coming. It is a visitation that is the result of a people that cries out and seeks him desperately. He comes in order to prepare the Church. Here, he sits down in order to refine. This means something done in detail, done with love and delicacy. A presence of fire is manifest, but it is not a destructive fire or a fire of wrath, but a fire that subtly burns off the dross.

We are going to see that the response to this treatment is the establishment of righteousness in the heart of His people, and the response of their children is an offering, an act of thanksgiving and worship that proceed from one of the foundations of the throne of God, righteousness.

Once the dross is removed and the gold of His children is shining, He can proceed to the judgment of wrath that will destroy his enemies and establish His throne.

Malachi said:

> And I will come near to you to JUDGMENT; and I will be a swift witness against the sorcerers, and against the adulterers, and against false swearers, and against those that oppress the hireling in his wages, the widow, and the fatherless, and that turn aside the stranger from his right, and fear not me, saith the LORD of hosts.
>
> —*Malachi 3:5*

My heart groans when I see so many of God's children attacked by witches, how they are defrauded and suffer injustices. They get sick, and even die, and their prayers appear not to have been heard. The attacks are so continual that many of the servants of the Lord are at the point of fainting.

The Lord has heard from heaven, people of God, and He is coming suddenly to His temple!

It is good that it is written that judgment begins in the house of God! But judgment does not come in the same measure upon those who are seeking to be clean and are judged, and upon those who do not have the fear of God in them.

Then they that feared the LORD spake often one to another: and the LORD hearkened, and heard it, and a book of remembrance was written before him for them that feared the LORD, and that thought upon his name.

And they shall be mine, saith the LORD of hosts, in that day when I make up my jewels; and I will spare them, as a man spareth his own son that serveth him.

Then shall ye return, and discern between THE RIGHTEOUS AND THE WICKED, between him that serveth God and him that serveth him not.

—*Malachi 3:16-18*

I Came To Judgment Before The Great Judge Of The Universe

It was 1998, and I was still trying to recover from the greatest battle that the Lord had taken me through, the ascent of Mount Everest. This is the highest mountain in the world and is the location of one of the most important seats upon the face of the earth of the Babylonian queen of heaven.

The risk was extremely high and the level of battle without equal. We saw the glory of God descend visibly, when He sat on the high places of the earth, and the fruit of that battle has been extraordinary. Brother Alberto Motessi told us of his surprise when he went to Nepal in 1998, the country in which Mt. Everest is located. He said that from a sparse population of six pastors in 1996, that in 1998 there was an alliance of 250 pastors, and they brought together for his crusade 150,000 believers.

Brother Morris Cerullo visited India shortly after our expedition. He told us that unprecedented things happened. God gave his ministry team access to television during his crusade named "Mission to the World," and revival broke out as never before seen in India.

To the north of Everest, in China, where several have lost their lives as martyrs smuggling in Bibles, today, there are Christian printing presses, authorized by the government in order to distribute the Word of God in China.

In Arabia, Pakistan, and Iran, while prayer teams from the "Women Aglow" visited these nations, shortly after our descent from Everest, they witnessed the great commotion in Arabia because the high hierarchy of Islam had a personal visitation from Jesus, revealing himself to them as the Messiah. And at Mecca they declared it to millions of Muslims.

We have glorious testimonies from nearly every nation surrounding the Himalayas. The veil that held the 10/40-window captive has been broken by millions of warriors that have united our prayers for this great liberation.

What I am trying to say is that God does not judge or submit the forces of evil, without first a deep cleansing from God of his warriors. Light dispels darkness, and light will also make our dross visible.

The most intense moments I have experienced with God followed this great battle.

Before entering into the testimony of my judgment, I want to copy part of the words that God revealed to the prophet Rick Joyner of the United States, in his book The Final Quest, the impressive story of when this great servant of God of our days was caught away to heaven.

He finds himself before the White Throne of God, and Jesus is talking to him:

"There is a lot that you need to understand about my judgments. When I judge, I am not seeking to condemn or to justify, but that my righteousness be established. My righteousness is only found in perfect union with me. Those are my just judgments, to bring man into union with me.

My Church is now dressed in disgrace, because there are no judges within her. And there are no judges because she does not know me as Judge yet. I am going to raise up judges, so that my people can know my judgments. They will not only decide between people and events, but they will bring uprightness and righteousness. This means that they will make every case line up according to what I am.

... I never come to take sides with anyone, but to take the authority and to put things in order. I appeared to Israel as the Captain of the army so they could enter to possess the Promised Land, and I will come again as the Captain of the army, because the Church is about to enter their Promised Land. When I do it I am going to remove all those who force my people to take sides between one and another. My Righteousness does not take sides.

... You must be able to see my righteousness in order to walk in My authority because righteousness and judgment are the foundation of My throne."

As I mentioned before, God had used me, together with a beautiful team, for one of the battles of greatest spiritual relevance that had ever been fought: Mount Everest. We knew that it was not due to anything special in us, but by

His grace and His mercy. We had been exposed to such an extraordinary level of light during the battle that, inevitably, our turn came to look at ourselves before that shining radiance of His throne.

The strongest and most important shaking of my Christian walk was coming to me, but it would bring the fruit of the establishment of righteousness in my life. The greater the level of light to which we are exposed, the greater the level of holiness required. The greater the calling, the greater is the light of His righteousness, and the greater also will be His dealing with us, which will conform us more and more to His image.

It was February of 1998. I had returned from a research trip in Turkey and in Rome, where God took us to study strategy in order to confront the queen of heaven. We had been in the jail where Paul was, and, kneeling there on the floor, the Lord spoke to me about the great price and about the level of cross that this battle required. During the whole return flight, I pondered the words of the Lord. In the balance was an undefined, but gigantic, level of suffering and, on the other side, seeing the fall of the stronghold that I most desired to see overthrown. And with it, the consequent liberation of millions of captives of the queen of heaven.

Without knowing very well what I was going to be confronted with, I told God that, whatever the cost, I wanted the liberty of all those souls. God would bring shortly what would also be one of the most important revelations of my life, "the relationship that exists between being a participant in the sufferings of Christ and producing the light and the authority that dispels the darkness," of which I write later in this book.

I found myself in deep prayer in my house, when a Man appeared before me with white, shining clothing. His face was like the sun, but I could see His eyes. They were like two peaceful lakes of blue water and a flame of fire shone through the depths of His gaze. It was Jesus. He took me by the right hand. In His look could be felt stability, combined with an abundance of love. We entered into a place (I don't know if in body or outside of the body). There was a spiral staircase built of stone. We began to descend. He did not say anything. As we went down, light was becoming more and more scarce, until reaching a point of total darkness. Noting the fear in my heart, He turned and said to me, "Don't be afraid. THIS IS ALSO ME." He did not say "I am here, too," but "This is also Me." I understood that He wanted to reveal something to me about Himself, that perhaps would not be easy to understand.

When we arrived at what would be the bottom, there was no light at all, only a luminous sign that said "Direction Loneliness." Although there was no light shining on it, I could see the Lord by the light that emanated from His face. He was looking at me with deep tenderness, as when one wants to infuse someone with courage. Then He added, "It is necessary for you to be here for a time for the work that I have prepared for you. While you are here, you will not be able to hear My voice, or see Me, but know that I will be here, and that I will not leave you nor forsake you, and at the appointed time, I will raise you to great glory."

Then He took a sheet of paper and, in front of me, He tore it into little pieces, and He said to me, "Do you see what I am doing? It is necessary that I do this with your life and with your ministry, but I am in control, and I will raise you in great glory," He repeated.

Then He disappeared and I found myself back in my house. I knew that something terrible was about to come upon my life, but I didn't know from what direction this hurricane would enter. I called the presbytery of the church and the intercessors, and I told them what had happened to me, so that they would prepare their hearts, and so that they would know that everything that would come was part of a divine design.

Two days later, the earthquake came. In a matter of hours, my whole world came apart. Chaos shook in every direction and, before I knew it, I had lost everything in my life.

It was difficult to reconcile all that was happening. I had lived a Christian life in the greatest holiness and uprightness that I understood, and suddenly, everything crumbled before my eyes. How could tragedy, slander, and treason beat so mercilessly against a life consecrated to God in such an unjust manner?

My life became an unending nightmare, and only the word of His visitation sustained me. Fortunately, no matter how many injustices and horrors the devil tried to bring about, the design of what God had prepared was so beautiful and so powerful. I would not exchange those months of cross and intense pain for anything.

God organized a glorious defense in order to preserve my life and my ministry. Dr. Morris Cerullo, Dr. Peter Wagner, and Dr. Rony Chaves closed ranks in a deployment of love, as I never knew it existed. If I had thought that these three men were worthy of great honor, now I believe it even more. Many are perhaps great in name, but true greatness shows itself in humility and love and in a life nailed to the cross of Calvary. To them were added many more from other nations, and God has been powerfully glorified.

For more than a year that the judgment of God lasted, my life was broken to the deepest levels. My twin sister suffered a sudden attack of multiple brain tumors that took her to the threshold of death and, from there, the Lord raised her up. Years later, the Lord called her to His presence. My home was violently destroyed. I wound up homeless, broke, and robbed of my possessions, and of my car, practically without friends. Those who I thought were the closest and most faithful, stabbed me in the back and left me alone. Others took sides with the lies of the devil and tried to tear the ministry into pieces, and I did not understand why.

God writes His books in a different way in heaven, and His wisdom is higher than ours.

> "It is necessary that through many trials you enter into the kingdom of God."
>
> —*Acts 14:22*

The revelation that God gave me to write this book is the product of the impressive visitations of God during my Judgment. And it is with deep thanks to my beloved husband in heaven, Jesus, that I can now tell the depths to which he carried me, and that, through a life of peace, it would have been impossible to understand. He never left me or abandoned me, and there were no lack of "Simons of

Cyrene" who assisted me in carrying the cross in the most difficult moments.

I also want to clarify that what happened to me is not what is going to happen to everyone who comes to judgment in mercy. What happened to me has to do with the design of God for my life, and with the level of light and holiness that I have to manifest in the call to which He has called me. And to break ground always involves an additional price, beyond that paid by those that walk upon ground already trodden.

5

PRINCIPLES OF THE KINGDOM II: CHRIST, A KINGDOM OF LIGHT

For God, who commanded the light to shine out of darkness, hath shined in our hearts, TO GIVE THE LIGHT OF THE KNOWLEDGE OF THE GLORY OF GOD IN THE FACE OF JESUS CHRIST.

—2 Corinthians 4:6

The kingdom of heaven is a kingdom in which everything is light. The magnificent light of God illuminates God's great city. There is no night. There is no possibility of darkness. Everything gleams; everything glistens and is extraordinarily crystalline, transparent, pure, and full of His glory.

... God is light, and in him is no darkness at all.

—*1 John 1:5*

It is the light that is going to allow us to know Him, to know the different dimensions and mysteries of His glory, that is going to carry us to an encounter with His face, with the countenance of Jesus Christ, that shines more than the sun in its zenith.

It is the light that is going to permit us to manifest Him in such a way that no darkness will prevail around us. This is the highest form of spiritual warfare I know, and the one that cannot be defeated.

To understand the principles of light goes much further than a positional doctrine, in which we are the light due to the simple fact that we have received salvation in Christ Jesus. If the millions of Christians that are upon the face of the earth produced the light that God designed, there would not be one single demon left upon this planet.

The problem is that we are light theologically, but we must become illuminated in such a degree in the knowledge of His glory that we become one who manifests his gleaming light.

The glory of God is about to be poured out as no other generation has seen it. Isaiah the prophet saw these unparalleled moments towards which the Church is moving.

Arise, shine; for thy light is come, and the glory of the LORD is risen upon thee.

For, behold, the darkness shall cover the earth, and gross darkness the people: but the LORD shall arise upon thee, and his glory shall be seen upon thee.

And the Gentiles shall come to thy light, and kings to the brightness of thy rising.

—*Isaiah 60:1-3*

Here the Lord is not talking about a mystical light that we say that we have, but that no one can see. Here the Lord says that there is a level of light related to His glory that will be seen by all, and that the very kings will desire it, and will follow it.

The prophet Joel also saw it, in the form of a glorious army of light that rises, conquering everything in its path.

… As the morning spread upon the mountains: a great people and a strong; there hath not been ever the like, neither shall be any more after it, even to the years of many generations.

—*Joel 2:2*

This is already beginning to happen. A people is being raised up all over the earth, that understands the light, God's designs, and that moves in a power such as has never been seen before.

In many places where God allows me to travel, I am finding people whose light goes beyond theology, people who are seeing His shining face and who are being transformed at dizzying speeds.

Light is a series of truths that manifest everything that Jesus is, in the same way in which light is diffracted into seven colors, but, all together, these colors produce white light. Likewise, the way in which each aspect of the light of Christ is being manifested, the light will increase in our life.

But we all, WITH OPEN FACE beholding as in a
glass the glory of the Lord, are changed into the same
image from glory to glory, even as by the Spirit of the
Lord.

—*2 Corinthians 3:18*

The knowledge of His glory is reached through a real
and vivid experience with the face of Jesus Christ.
WE ARE TRANSFORMED IN HIM, IN THE
MEASURE IN WHICH WE LOOK AT HIM, IN THE
MEASURE THAT CHRIST REVEALS HIMSELF TO
US.

From the small, fragile awareness of His presence in the
beginning of our Christian life, to the glorious ecstasy of
seeing Him face to face, the experiences that we have with
Him are what produce the glorious changes that are going
to conform us to His image.

This is light: knowing Him. Light is knowing His
progressive, wonderful revelation until everything is full
of His kingdom and glory, as the waters cover the sea.
Many say that Christianity is not a religion, but a personal
relationship with Jesus. And this is true, but the reality is
that not everyone has this relationship. Relationship means
when you can look at someone in their eyes, you hold their
hands, and they can hold yours, to be able to give them a
hug, listen to their voice, to share with them, and that they
share with you, the intimate parts of their hearts. A true
relationship is not an intellectual knowledge or an emotion.
To know Him is to experience Him every day, not only
knowing about Him, reading the Word. And what is true
is that, unfortunately, many people have a religion, and not
a relationship.

Everything that is revealed to us is a product of light. The nature of light is that everything is seen in lustrous clarity.

That is why Paul prayed:

That the God of our Lord Jesus Christ, the Father of glory, may give unto you the spirit of wisdom and revelation in the knowledge of him:

The eyes of your understanding being ENLIGHT-ENED; that ye may know what is the hope of his calling, and what the riches of the glory of his inheritance in the saints.

—Ephesians 1:17-18

To enlighten means to fill with light or insight. As such, we see that the revelation of Christ in us has to do with the level of light in which we move.

The word tells us that there are different levels of relationship with Christ. One was the relationship of the disciples, another, the relationship of the three that were at the transfiguration, and another level, the one that the disciple John, the beloved, had.

We see different levels of glory mentioned by Paul, when he talks about how the resurrection will be; one is the glory of the sun, another, the glory of the moon, and another, the glory of the stars. Likewise, when we are transformed into our incorruptible bodies.

Following this same line of thought, there are also within the body of Christ different levels of light and, as a consequence, different levels of revelation.

Where does the knowledge of light come from? How can we pass from a positional light at the level of salvation, to a true level of light that dispels all darkness?

God spoke to Job, and he said:

Where is the way where light dwelleth? And as for darkness, where is the place thereof,

That thou shouldest take it to the bound thereof, and that thou shouldest know the paths to the house thereof?

Knowest thou it, because thou wast then born? Or because the number of thy days is great?

—*Job 38:19-21*

Light Is Truth

Jesus is the light that came to this world.

In him was life; and the life was the light of men.

And the light shineth in darkness; and the darkness comprehended it not.

—*John 1:4-5*

The life contained in Jesus is what produces light. But it was necessary that this life was poured out as a living sacrifice, so that it would produce the effect of Light.

Jesus did not conquer the devil with the anointing that was upon Him, or with the miracles, or living a holy life. It was on the cross of Calvary, where He conquered the forces of evil. It was there that every victory was consummated. And it is there, too, where darkness could not prevail against the light.

The cross, one of the least preached messages in churches today, is the place of bounty, of manifestation, and of fulfillment. Understanding the cross, is opening the door that is going to carry us to the hidden mysteries of God, to the most priceless treasures of His kingdom.

It is in the cross where the repositories of the most extraordinary wisdom of God are conjugated. The revelation of his infinite love is there, the culmination of the hidden truths of His humiliation, are drunk at the cross. The entrance to the highest levels of light, of resurrection, are there, too, as well as the door to the highest dimensions of His truth.

There is no greater treasure than to learn to submerse ourselves in the cross, in each part of His excellent sacrifice, of his sufferings. There are rivers of living waters there, torrents of revelation, that is His shining light. Paul understood this, and that is why he gave up everything:

> But what things were gain to me, those I counted loss for Christ.

> Yea doubtless, and I count all things but loss for the excellency of the knowledge of Christ Jesus my Lord: for whom I have suffered the loss of all things, and do count them but dung, that I may win Christ.
> —*Philippians 3:7-8*

> That I may know him, and the power of his resurrection, and the fellowship of his sufferings, being made conformable unto his death;

> If by any means I might attain unto the resurrection of the dead.

Not as though I had already attained, either were already perfect: but I follow after, if that I may apprehend that for which also I am apprehended of Christ Jesus.

—Philippians 3:10-12

Everything that is so carefully hidden in each drop of His shed blood, and in the water of life that comes mixed with this vital fluid, is so deep and so wonderful!

Paul lived this truth, and it was his burning desire to live crucified together with Christ so that everything that Jesus was, would manifest itself through his being.

Always bearing about in the body the dying of the Lord Jesus, that the life also of Jesus might be made manifest in our body.

—2 Corinthians 4:10

Paul said:

For our light affliction, which is but for a moment, worketh for us a far more exceeding and eternal weight of glory;

While we look not at the things which are seen, but at the things which are not seen: for the things which are seen are temporal; but the things which are not seen are eternal.

—2 Corinthians 4:17-18

How did light begin to produce itself through the cross? Jesus had to become just like us in order to be able to be our intercessor and our high priest. For that He needed to be taken to the place of disgrace and reproach. Calvary was not a glorious place, as the artists of the Renaissance paint it. It was a place of evil, a place beside the city dump, where the most slippery and disgusting criminals were executed. This is the place where He chose to die for us.

It was there that He was counted among the transgressors. This means that He was seen as one of them, one just the same as us.

On the cross, He exposed sin. He carried in His body the decree that was against us. In every blow to His face, in every injury to His body, in every lash of the whip, in every wound, in the holes made by the nails, in His face scratched by thorns, are inscribed the sins of us all.

His body, nailed to the cross, was a decree of all our transgressions, out in the open and exposed to the light of day.

The cross is the exposition of sin. The cross is to come to reproach, to be stripped naked, to be exposed.

It is here where the vessel is broken, and the light begins to manifest itself.

This is what destroyed the devil, the impressive humiliation of Christ.

Stripped naked of His clothing, removing sin from every hidden place, He openly exposed it on the cross.

Today, the Church says it is light, but light cannot manifest itself in hiding. And what am I referring to when I say the Church is in hiding?

The Word clearly states:

> This then is the message which we have heard of him, and declare unto you, that God is light, and in him is no darkness at all.

If we say that we have fellowship with him, and walk in darkness, we lie, and do not the truth:

But if we walk in the light, as he is in the light, we have fellowship one with another, and the blood of Jesus Christ his Son cleanseth us from all sin.

—*1 John 1:5-7*

If we see these passages in the light of the truth, we realize that something is wrong in the Church today, because the greatest sin in the Church around the world is precisely that there is no fellowship one with another. The divisions, the jealousy, envy, and the lack of love is what I see abound from even the heart of the local church. How then can we say that we are light?

Notice in what moment it is that the blood of Jesus Christ cleanses us from sin: when we walk in light. And, as a consequence of walking in the light, we have communion one with another.

The passage of John continues, saying:

If we say that we have no sin, we deceive ourselves, and the truth is not in us.

If we confess our sins, he is faithful and just to forgive us our sins, and to cleanse us from all unrighteousness.

If we say that we have not sinned, we make him a liar, and his word is not in us.

—*1 John 1:8-10*

In the epistle of James, we also find this word "confess:"

Confess your faults one to another...

—*James 5:16*

Let's go to the root of things and we will understand to what the scripture is referring.

When Martin Luther, the great reformer of the 16th century, nailed his Ninety-five Theses on the door of the church, one of them said: No, to public confession of sins. Number one, we must understand that the theses of the Reformation ARE NOT THE BIBLE, and there are several terrible errors within them and one of them is this one.

Let's understand that Luther came from a Catholic background, during the darkest period that the world has experienced. The abuses that were committed in that era— selling forgiveness in order to buy heaven, taking advantage of confessions in order to take people's money—were atrocious. Luther, who received the light of salvation by grace through faith, hated the horrors that were being committed at that time, supposedly in the Name of God. He reacted to his time, but this does not mean to say that he had the entire truth.

The confession of sins between one and another, as shown by James, is the genuine form of liberation and deep cleansing of our soul. The same etymology of the word "confess" means "to speak publicly." We use this same word when someone comes to salvation and we tell them to make a public declaration of faith:

> For with the heart man believeth unto righteousness; and with the mouth confession is made unto salvation.
>
> —*Romans 10:10*

This means that he must speak before everyone about what he believes about Jesus.

Why then, when the same word is used for the confession of sin, we think that it must be done in a secret manner and only before God, so that no one knows what we have done? (Obviously, there are attitudes and minor daily faults that we can confess to God).

If Jesus was stripped naked of all of His clothing and the sin of the world was exposed to public light, and He publicly defeated in this way principalities and powers, why do we want to have victory in hiding?

How can the sin of the Church be remitted, if the sin does not come out into the light? Didn't Jesus say, speaking about the kingdom:

> And when he had said this, he breathed on them, and saith unto them, Receive ye the Holy Ghost:
>
> Whose soever sins ye remit, they are remitted unto them; and whose soever sins ye retain, they are retained.
>
> —*John 20:22-23*

What does this mean? Why have we eliminated this from our doctrine? Why does the proverb say:

> He that covereth his sins shall not prosper: but whosoever confesseth and forsaketh them shall have mercy.
>
> —*Proverbs 28:13*

Let's be honest and let's look at the condition of the Church around the world. Isn't it full of sin, of people who cannot prosper, of people beat up by the devil, robbed and humiliated, of people who want to reach the kingdom, but can't, due to so much erroneous doctrine about which we have all been mistaken?

The fact is that the ministries that I have seen prosper, are those that in some way have someone to whom they confess their sins. They may have done it because they wanted to be free or helped, or because they have burdens that they could no longer bear, or because the attack of the devil in the area of sickness or in finances was insufferable. Then they looked for someone and they opened their heart. It was at that moment that they could be truly cleansed, and they began to prosper.

What does history tell us? Every great revival has begun with men and women who understood this principle. Every time the glory of God has come upon a place, it is because a wave of repentance and confession of sin has preceded it.

Those who have read or heard Charles Finney speak, say that in his meetings he spoke so strongly about sin that literally the flames of hell were felt under their feet.

When Aimee Semple McPherson preached, people fell in ecstasy, some saw heaven and others felt that they were swallowed by hell, and they cried out, repenting of their sins.

Confession is the way to come to the light, it is coming to the place where the devil can no longer threaten you and where his accusations are destroyed. The devil does not have any power upon your life when you truly come to the light, when you come to reproach, as Jesus came to reproach. When you strip yourself naked of the clothing of sin, exposing it to the light, as Jesus was stripped naked and exposed Himself instead of the wicked, if He went to the place of shame, why do we want to protect ourselves, so that no one thinks badly about us?

> He that saith he abideth in him ought himself also so to walk, even as he walked.
>
> *—1 John 2:6*

> Let this mind be in you, which was also in Christ Jesus:

> Who, being in the form of God, thought it not robbery to be equal with God:

> But made himself of no reputation, and took upon him the form of a servant, and was made in the likeness of men:

> And being found in fashion as a man, he humbled himself, and became obedient unto death, even the death of the cross.
>
> *—Philippians 2:5-8*

Why is it humiliating going to the death of the cross? It is because this is where everyone looks at you as being the basest. This was the place that Jesus chose. He preferred to be counted with the sinners, instead of with the great men of this world. Today, if there is a fallen brother, or a misunderstood or defeated brother, and someone joins him in order to help and love him, the advice that you are given is: "You had better stay away from him. Your testimony could be tarnished if you are seen with brothers like that one." But Jesus preferred that they hide their faces from him, that they considered him beaten by God, to be considered a man without reputation, despised, and cast out by man, scorned and without esteem, but loving and walking in the truth.

Speaking the truth about ourselves, recognizing our sins, our failures, our erroneous decisions, is walking in the light. Confessing the sin to others keeps us humble, and it is highly honorable before God. He who humbles himself will be exalted, and he who exalts himself will be humbled.

We are all human. We all make mistakes. We all sin, and we can all be forgiven and redeemed by the redemptive grace of Christ.

Repenting and speaking their sins was not a problem for the early Church or for the men of God in the Old Testament. There was a very different understanding about what this meant. They were always aware of the preeminence of God; what God thought was the most important thing, not what man thought. Today, the reverse appears to be the case.

You do not see, for example, a tremendous fight between Peter and the authors of the Gospels, because they published, for all time, his sin when he denied Jesus. I believe they discussed it with Peter, and he must have said, "Yes, of course, write all of this. It is necessary that everything that I did remains as an example for others." Likewise, when Luke wrote about Peter, saying that he was worthy of condemnation due to his behavior with the Gentiles.

You do not see that Paul hid his sin, but he talks about himself as a cast off. You do not see David strip Samuel of his post for writing and making his sin public. David was a man after God's own heart. Confessions of his sins and failures are seen everywhere in the Psalms. He himself wrote about it in order for his confession to be published and so everyone could read about how he felt before God.

Have mercy upon me, O God, according to thy loving kindness: according unto the multitude of thy tender mercies blot out my transgressions.

Wash me thoroughly from mine iniquity, and cleanse me from my sin.

For I acknowledge my transgressions: AND MY SIN IS EVER BEFORE ME.

Against thee, thee only, have I sinned, and done this evil in thy sight: THAT THOU MIGHTEST BE JUSTIFIED WHEN THOU SPEAKEST, AND BE CLEAR WHEN THOU JUDGEST.

Behold, I was shapen in iniquity, and in sin did my mother conceive me.

BEHOLD, THOU DESIREST TRUTH IN THE INWARD PARTS: AND IN THE HIDDEN PART THOU SHALT MAKE ME TO KNOW WISDOM.

Purge me with hyssop, and I shall be clean: wash me, and I shall be whiter than snow.

Make me to hear joy and gladness; that the bones which thou hast broken may rejoice.

Hide thy face from my sins, and blot out all mine iniquities.

Create in me a clean heart, O God; and renew a right spirit within me.

Cast me not away from thy presence; and take not thy holy spirit from me.

Restore unto me the joy of thy salvation; and uphold
me with thy free spirit.

THEN WILL I TEACH TRANSGRESSORS THY
WAYS; AND SINNERS SHALL BE CONVERTED
UNTO THEE.

—Psalm 51:1b-13

Notice how the perspective, David's point of view, is so
different from that of the Church of this century. For David,
it was not important how he was seen before men, but that
God were recognized as just in His word and considered
pure in His judgment.

David knew that if he humbled himself and made his
sin public, writing about it and allowing it to remain for all
time, God would be exalted. And, as a reward, He would
allow David to preach the truth, and the people would
really come, repentant, to God's feet and with conviction
of sin.

At least this is what my soul longs for, to preach Jesus
and that people would truly change their ways, that His
presence within me would be so strong that they would
desire it with all their hearts.

One day God said to me, "Ana, IN HEAVEN, THE
BOOKS ARE WRITTEN DIFFERENTLY THAN ON
THE EARTH: LIVE YOUR LIFE ACCORDING TO
THE BOOKS WRITTEN IN HEAVEN."

Here, we can appear that we are immaculate saints, who
never commit any error. And men will put us on high and
will write about us. But in heaven, we are seen and written
about differently.

Next to each one of us, there is an angel that writes, day
and night, the book of our lives.

> And I saw the dead, small and great, stand before
> God; and the books were opened: and another book
> was opened, which is the book of life: and the dead
> were judged out of those things which were written
> in the books, according to their works.
>
> —*Revelation 20:12*

Today, the calls to repentance that are made in churches, are considered to be somewhat shameful. Unbelievers go up along with a few others, and the rest of the church remains seated, as if we all believed that in all of those immovable people, there is no more sin.

It is more important to us for men to think we are "perfect," than what God is seeing in us.

For God, there is no more wonderful moment than when we run to the altar to confess our sins. To Him, it is the most beautiful party. When we confess our sins and we repent, there is a party of angels in heaven. To God, it is not shameful that we come and we repent every single day, if necessary. Every time that we do it, He is recognized as just in His word, and pure in his judgment.

We sin in so many ways, oh, saints of God! Every time we limit the Spirit, we sin. Every time we put in place our religious methods, and we restrict the liberty of what God wants to do, we sin. Every time we could move by faith, but instead, we choose human methods in order to resolve things, we sin. Every time we accept any reproach against a brother, when we show preferential treatment to people, we sin. When we see our brother in need and we close our heart to him, we sin. Every time we choose to protect our reputation instead of taking steps of love, we sin. (And loving, sometimes, has a very high price.) When we forget about the orphans and the widows, even those within our own churches, we sin. When our material desires in this world are our priorities, more than the work of God or remembering the poor, we sin. Then add to this list jealousy, envy, strife, division, judging others, and all of the works of the flesh, together with terrible abominations.

Do you really believe, beloved reader, that someone can remain seated in their pew because really he has no more sin? Isn't it time to please God and to speak the truth one to another, and take off our masks that, deep inside, everyone knows we are wearing?

The truth is, light dispels darkness. When you decide to stand in the light and to speak the truth, no matter the cost, when you have sinned and you have made mistakes, when you have done something that, in the eyes of others, is wrong, and you decide to speak the truth anyway, then God will shine through you.

This is not easy. The whisper that is most often heard from the devil is, "Protect yourself! Don't let them think poorly of you. Remember that you are a leader, and you are an example of holiness! You had better arrange things so that you look good before men."

The answer of God to this is, "No, get behind me Satan! If I am a leader, I must teach my people the truth, honesty, and humility. I want to be the example that will make them strong before God, even though men say all kinds of bad things against me, telling lies. I choose to please God and that in my book in heaven it be written, 'She honored God before men,' rather than to protect myself on the earth and that it be written above, 'She dishonored God. She chose the lie and was praised by men.'"

As I said before, this is not easy. It requires a level of cross, of understanding that the death and the reproach of "me," assists life and resurrection. Even though they reject you here, and persecute you, great is your reward in heaven, because you chose Him before yourself.

This is a principle of the kingdom that has to become alive within us.

> For whosoever will save his life shall lose it; but whosoever shall lose his life for my sake and the gospel's, the same shall save it.
>
> —*Mark 8:35*

The people of the kingdom have to be a living message. It has to be true, even though we don't like the truth about ourselves.

Exposing one's self is nailing one's self with Christ to the cross, it is entering into a position of light where you cannot be defeated. And when religious spirits nail you to the cross for speaking the truth, they will be helping you to be in the only place where power is produced, and from where light arises that dispels darkness.

This is the true light, that, when it is present in the waters of the world, it attracts all of the fish towards itself.

It is nailed to the cross, humbling yourself, where the shining face of the Beloved becomes visible. As David said,

> For with thee is the fountain of life: in thy light shall we see light.
>
> —*Psalm 36:9*

It is there, when you are looking at Him face to face, that you can see all of the impurity of your being, covered by His grace and by His forgiveness, and you can proclaim like the Shunammite woman,

I am black, but comely, O ye daughters of Jerusalem, as the tents of Kedar, as the curtains of Solomon.

Look not upon me, because I am black, because the sun hath looked upon me...

—Song of Solomon 1:5-6

When the sun of righteousness looks at you, when He makes His face shine upon you, is when you can see the clay of which we are made, and say:

But we have this treasure in earthen vessels, that the excellency of the power may be of God, and not of us.

—2 Corinthians 4:7

In the kingdom of darkness, the devil knows perfectly well who is light, who is nailed to the cross, and remains nailed to the cross. He also knows those who say they are light, but their light is darkness covered by masks, that have the appearance of godliness, but deny the power thereof.

For this reason there are so many wounded in spiritual warfare; not because Christ hasn't given us the power, but because many want to go to war without having to live the cross that defeats the devil.

Light Is Love

This is perhaps one of the most important segments of this book. And it is the essence of an intense cry of REFOR-MATION that is going forth from heaven throughout the whole earth.

In the beginning was the Word, and the Word was with God, and the Word was God.

The same was in the beginning with God.

All things were made by him; and without him was not any thing made that was made.

In him was life; AND THE LIFE WAS THE LIGHT OF MEN.

And the light shineth in darkness; and the darkness conquered it not.

—John 1:1-5

As we see in this passage, light is the visible manifestation of the life of Jesus. This word was made flesh and dwelt among us. Life itself left the Father in order to live in the blood contained in the body of Jesus.

Light and life, circulated in that glorious blood. It is written:

For the life of the flesh is in the blood...

—Leviticus 17:11

That is the same blood that would be shed due to His love for all of us.

Light, life, and love are intimately bound together, and the one is nothing without the other, and the other without the one.

There is no light outside of love, nor love outside of light, and these two are the same life of God manifesting itself.

THE SECRET TO SHINE IS TO LOVE!

For God so loved the world, that he gave his only begotten Son, that whosoever believeth in him should not perish, but have everlasting life.

—John 3:16

Love is the vital principle of light, and, as such, the origin of all revelation. The greater the understanding of love, the more light will come, and the more light, we will also have more revelation.

John was the disciple of love. No one knew better the love of God that he did. And it was to him that the greatest revelation of the New Testament was given, Revelation.

Paul was caught away to the third heaven, but due to the revelations, a messenger from Satan was given to him to buffet him. Nevertheless, it was not necessary to send John this type of affliction, because he knew love, and love is infinitely humble.

Revelation is a product of love. Revelation is light. Everything that is revealed is revealed because light has illuminated it.

Paul writes to the Colossians and says:

That their hearts might be comforted, being knit together in love, and unto all riches of the full assurance of understanding, to the acknowledgment of the mystery of God, and of the Father, and of Christ;

In whom are hid all the treasures of wisdom and knowledge.

—*Colossians 2:2-3*

Without love it is impossible to penetrate the sphere of light and of the deepest revelation that awaken the glorious mysteries of the divinity.

The reason why we just receive revelation as with an eyedropper is because we live isolated under a structure of selfishness, of self-protection, with barriers that isolate us

from one another. This is darkness that covers our heart.
He who is in darkness can only see his own needs.

The Greatest Force In The Universe

God had begun to speak to me in a deep way, since the
time that we had trained to climb Mount Everest. We were
waging spiritual warfare on the highest mountain in Peru,
"the Huascarán," a peak of 7,000 meters (or 22,965 ft.) high.
The devil, attempting to impede the order of God to take
the high places of the earth, sent a sickness to my heart
that made mountain climbing impossible, at least at these
heights. But God had me well trained not to pay atten-
tion to what the devil says or does. I had a divine mission,
designed and spoken by God, and nothing would stop me,
even if I could feel death itself upon me.

The pain in my heart began to be extremely intense as we
climbed, so much so that I had to stop every ten steps, until
it let up a little, and then I could go another stretch. The
time came when I had to grab onto a high rock because I
literally felt that I was going to die. I couldn't take even one
more step. I had asked my heart for a superhuman effort,
and it was at the limit of its resistance.

The weight of an irrecoverably botched mission filled my
eyes with tears. Then I cried out to God, one more time,
and I asked Him, "Where is the power for victory? I have
confessed every Scripture I know. I have pled the power of
Your blood and of Your stripes, the power of Your name
and of Your Spirit. Please, speak to me!"

At that precise moment, something extraordinary
happened. A dense cloud of light began to descend from
the heights of Huascarán. It was like a thick, gigantic veil

of brilliant, transparent gold that began to cover everything. I stared at it in ecstasy, while the presence of God was felt everywhere. It continued coming down slowly, until it enveloped me completely.

Then, I heard a voice that came out from that radiance that spoke to me, and said, "It is My love, daughter. It is My love. My love is the greatest force in the universe. For love, you will do things that you wouldn't do for any other reason."

Then, that thick, splendid veil was filled with faces. They were millions of Peruvian faces. With a deep, sweet voice He said, "Look at how much I love them! Look at how much I love them!"

Suddenly, like an incredible injection of life, the power of love filled me completely. All of my being filled with vigor, as if those millions of hopeful faces in Jesus had become a part of me, and I would do anything for them.

The mountain still shone when I began to climb again. A new, great power was upon me. I knew that we would win the battle. This was one of the most glorious battles of my life and one in which a true reformation began within my being.

This was only the beginning. God would continue an intense labor, working in my heart. During the year that the intense affliction of my life lasted, God taught me that love is of divine origin. Love is God. Love is: that He loved us first.

Just as in the book of Proverbs (chapter 8), we see wisdom acting in the form of a person, likewise love is a Person and wants to be treated as such. This Person is Jesus, but it is the part of His being that is above all of His attributes and greatness.

It is in this part of Himself that the fullness of God manifests itself. Paul says,

For in him dwelleth all the fullness of the Godhead bodily.

—*Colossians 2:9*

What gives the fullness is not some great anointing of power, or the greatness of a ministry, or the size of a church. Only love gives fullness.

Love is of spiritual origin, since love is God. It is not something that comes from a deep emotion, nor is it something of our will, as I have heard so many say, "Love is a decision." Love is not a decision, which is solely a mechanism of the soul.

Love is a Person, who wants to exist through you, who wants to love through you, who wants to unite with you in your spirit, and flood with fullness your entire being.

It is in the love of God where heaven and earth are mixed and united.

The world is made in three dimensions: length, width, and depth, and, within these three dimensions, everything that was created exists. But when the Bible speaks about the love of Jesus, four dimensions appear. Length, width, depth (the earth) and add height, which is heaven united with the earth in Christ Jesus.

This is the most powerful anointing that has already begun to descend upon the face of the planet, the anointing of His love.

A foundational anointing will flow upon the true apostles and prophets of the last days. These men are the wise master builders, designed by God to restore to the Church its true foundation, "the love of God," which is the chief corner-stone of the revelation of Christ.

The present day Church is founded on doctrines, doctrines of baptism, doctrines of dead works, doctrines of gifts, etc, etc.

I have looked through manual after manual about disci-pleship, and of those that have come into my hands, which are many, I have yet to find one that teaches the believer to lay his foundation upon love.

Love is not an option; it is the highest, and the only commandment, that Jesus gave us, because love is the life in His blood, which mixes together and flows throughout His body. Without love, the body cannot exist as such; it is only dried bones, scattered about and dead.

A Trip Inside The Heart Of God

I saw many glorious things during the time in which God afflicted my life, and one of them was during an ecstasy that lasted seven days on the island of Patmos. The Lord took me there in order to teach me the depths of His love, in which He wants to bathe the earth in this next millennium.

It was September of 1999 when I arrived at the small island on the Aegean Sea, where the beloved disciple had his greatest experience. From the time that I arrived, I knew that the heavens remained open, and the presence of God could be felt everywhere.

The island is practically virgin, and the forest in which John prayed is still intact. It was there where I set up camp in order to live one of the most life-transforming visitations that Jesus has permitted me to experience.

From the beginning, the Spirit of God caught me up in an ecstasy in which He literally brought me inside His heart. First, I had the strange sensation of being in front of the cross, as if I were in John's very shoes. I saw Jesus hanging from the cross. All of his wounds made my own body ache. I saw his bruised, deformed face, and I wanted to throw myself upon Him and clean, with kisses of love, the blood that ran down His cheeks. He looked into my eyes. His eyes were almost swollen shut and were glassy with the look of the death that was beginning to invade them. Even yet He looked at me and He filled me with His love.

From His eyes flowed silent words that said to me, "Thank you for being with Me in My pain. Thank you for not leaving Me alone. The Father and the Spirit have distanced Themselves because of the sin that is upon Me. Your love gives Me strength, beloved. Stay with Me until the end."

"Yes! Yes!" My heart shouted, or John's heart. I don't know, it was like being mixed together with him.

Suddenly, the body of the Lord began to tremble, and a deep, distressed cry left his lips. I felt that it pierced through me. "My beloved, my beloved! Don't go!" shouted my soul, as the cry of His death resonated within me, like a deafening bell. It had been printed upon my soul, and I could not stop hearing it.

The earth began to shake, and the heavens were darkened. There was confusion everywhere. Shouts were heard. I was paralyzed, like John. I was living everything that John felt. My eyes were fixed upon Jesus. I could not believe that my beloved was there…dead.

The sound of the armor of the Roman army brought me back to my senses. With violence and without any mercy whatsoever, they approached the two hung thieves, and they broke their legs. But when they came to Jesus, since they saw that He was already dead, they stopped. One of the soldiers kept looking at me with disgust, and then he turned. With his spear, he pierced the heart of my beloved.

There, right in front of me, I saw Jesus' heart open, and blood and water came out of his side. "I, John, am the one giving testimony of this."

While I looked at the wound in His side, the heart of Jesus changed into the heart of the Father. Suddenly, I saw as if it were a door that opened in this great, vital organ, and the Spirit took me inside.

Inside it was like a tabernacle with walls of flesh. There was a courtyard, a holy place, and the holy of holies. I spent four whole days there. Each part of this impressive place was full of wounds and open lacerations. They were different and of differentiating gravity. These were the marks of pain that remain recorded in the heart of the Father due to sin. Sin tears His insides apart in a very painful way. There inside, there were sins that affected the courtyard, others the holy place, and others, where I saw the most serious wounds, arrived at the holy of holies.

During the days that I spent there, the Lord spoke to me about each one of His wounds. I spent a lot of time in the holy of holies. There the pain was the most intense. I asked the Holy Spirit what these wounds were. What kinds of sins were so horrible that they caused this depth of damage inside the Father's heart? He told me, "These are the sins against love, in any of its forms; divisions, hatred among the brethren, slander, treason, criticisms, when they attack and destroy each other, when, full of jealousy, they persecute one another, when they annihilate the fallen, and they hate among themselves. These are the sins that wound the Father the most," He added.

Then God showed me the impressive holiness of love. God is love. And His love shines with dazzling brilliance, because it is holy. This holiness emanates from His own heart and is, in itself, the holy of holies.

It was an extremely reverential glory that was before me, while His love surrounded and consumed me, like an intensely powerful fire that filled me in a gigantic wave of life, of grace, and of mercy. It was impressively pure, holy, and infinitely holy. It was the heart of God.

As a truth that was impressed upon my spirit, the Lord spoke to me about the holy of holies of His own heart. This is the place of complete, full fellowship, of the deepest intimacy between God and man. It is where the fullness designed to fill our heart finds it highest manifestation. It is there that our heart finds total and perfect union with God.

The Word became alive within me.

… Rooted and grounded in love,

May be able to comprehend with all saints what is the breadth, and length, and depth, and height;

And to know the love of Christ, which passeth knowledge, that ye might be filled with all the fullness of God.

—*Ephesians 3:17-19*

Then I heard a voice that came forth from the midst of the glorious holiness, and it said to me, "My love is holy, and there is no possibility of holiness outside of My love."

Holiness has nothing to do with religious conduct. It is a matter of love, of founding ourselves on God, of giving our lives for others, as He gave His life for us. Holiness is to love from the glorious sacrifice of the cross, where the total negation of self is found, so that love, which gives everything on behalf of others, can express itself. The more that we stir ourselves into that glorious essence between our spirit and His Spirit, the more I cease being "me" in order to change into "us", loving Him through loving others, the more I am drawn nearer to His holiness.

After that, he showed me the temple of love in a marriage. This is the spiritual place where two souls bond together with God. It is in the marital bed where holiness and pure love are bound together. What happens there is intimately tied to the heart of God and is infinitely powerful. Then He showed me the terrible abomination of adultery and of sexual perversion. He who perverts the marriage bed, touches the holy of holies. He or she is touching the holiness of God in the very area of His heart. It is as if he or she were to allow pigs into the holiest place of God.

Sins against love, in any of its forms, touch the most delicate and sensitive area of the heart of the Father.

Love is not an option. Outside of love there is only thick darkness. And it is terribly painful how we wound God.

He that saith he is in the light, and hateth his brother, is in darkness even until now.

He that loveth his brother abideth in the light, and there is none occasion of stumbling in him.

But he that hateth his brother is in darkness, and walketh in darkness, and knoweth not whither he goeth, because that darkness hath blinded his eyes.

—1 John 2:9-11

This is the greatest tragedy that I have seen in the churches around the world, that the people do not know how to love, or how to give to others selflessly in love.

And hereby we do know that we know him, if we keep his commandments.

He that saith, I know him, and keepeth not his commandments, is a liar, and the truth is not in him.

But whosoever keepeth his word, in him verily is the love of God perfected...

—1 John 2:3-5a

And this is the word that Jesus gave us to keep:

A new commandment I give unto you, That ye love one another; as I have loved you, that ye also love one another.

BY THIS SHALL ALL MEN KNOW THAT YE ARE MY DISCIPLES, IF YE HAVE LOVE ONE TO ANOTHER.

—John 13:34-35

Could a lost world needing love, a world that shouts in its loneliness and in its horrible emptiness, really see us as disciples of Christ, when there is so much selfishness, so much division and so much judging, and criticism within our ranks? Will we perhaps have the courage to see the truth and to cry out for understanding of the highest concept on the universe: the love of God, that is much greater and deeper than we can even imagine?

The Spirit Of God Is Choking Inside The Body

When my sister, Mercedes, became filled with brain tumors, during all of the shaking that beat upon us, the Lord spoke to me in a tremendous way.

For more than a year, she found herself connected to tubes all over her body. They were practically keeping her alive artificially. The only parts of her that were working were her spirit, her mind, and one hand.

One day, when I went to see her, she was rolled up into a ball. She had turned into nothing. She signaled me to bring her a piece of paper and a pen in order to write something. Her eyes were full of tears. With a lot of effort she traced a few words that said, "It is so hard to live in a body that does not know how to die." I could see how her spirit was choking inside of her paralyzed body.

It was so difficult to contain my cry, since this had to do with the closest person to me, my identical twin. Mercedes and I came from the same cell and divided into two. And the love that we feel one for another is a love that is known only by those of us who are identical twins.

The pain I felt upon seeing her like that was killing me, but that day it was worse when I arrived home, and I got into the presence of God.

I began to hear the Holy Spirit, crying inconsolably. I asked Him, startled, "What is the matter, Holy Spirit? Why are you crying?"

He answered me, "The condition of your sister is a sign. This is how the body of Christ is living: artificially! Many have the name that they are alive, but they are already dead. Others want to survive, but without Me. And they have little time left, and I am choking in a disjointed, sick body."

I cried a long time, crying out to God for His body and asking the Holy Spirit's forgiveness.

Little by little, through terrible operations, the tumors were removed. As she was being surrounded with love and fervent prayer, by intercessors that gave themselves to conquer death itself, she began to recover feeling and her mobility.

Then the Spirit spoke to me again and said, "This is how it will be in this third millennium. I have designed operations in which I will remove the religious, fleshly tumors that have My body paralyzed. Some tumors will come out with the simple manifestation of my Spirit of Truth, that will bring repentance to My servants. These are the tumors that come out easily because they are not lodged in the flesh. But there are other tumors that I will remove through surgery, which are so rooted to the flesh that I cannot remove them without taking the flesh with them. The tumors I am talking about are deceiving spirits of division, of pride, and religious spirits that have gotten into My body, and the flesh are the ministers who have fallen victim of them.

Jesus' Loneliness

God created man from the depths of His heart and from the very fountain of love.

Every man is a spirit that came from God. We came from Him, but not from any part of Him. God, being complete in Himself, and in the fullness of the love that flowed within the very Trinity, He decided to pull from Himself a part of His own heart and to create from there mankind.

God would never again be complete in Himself in the area of love. He had created a being made from Himself. His heart was now in the hands of a beloved being that could fill it with the joy of an indescribable love, or could also destroy it with pain and scorn.

We were made in the image and likeness of God, and our heart was formed in the design of His own heart.

God created man with a heart that needed His Creator in order to feel complete. But He put another empty place inside of man. "It is not good for man to be alone." He created a wonderful "incomplete feeling" inside of man that can only be filled at the level of the soul with someone that empties their soul inside of him, each one becoming complete with the other, his beloved.

This is but the reflection of what God did with Himself. He also determined for His own heart, that wonderful incomplete feeling, that only finds its fullness when His beloved, the Church, empties herself into Him in order to bind her heart with His as one spirit. "Father, I ask that they would be one in Us, as You are one in Me and I in You." (Jesus, John 17:21-22, paraphrased)

The foundation of the universe and of all creation is love. Everything was created due to this glorious decision in the heart of God.

God determined to love us, and this means He made Himself need this love, your love and my love. Could God

NEED something? Only someone who does not under-stand love would say no. Doesn't the Shunammite woman in the Song of Solomon say,

> I charge you, O daughters of Jerusalem, if ye find my beloved, that ye tell him, that I am sick of love.
>
> —*Song of Solomon 5:8*

And her beloved only cries out because she is coming to him. "Make me hear your voice," he cries out, with a heart thirsty for her love.

To love is to understand, from our inner most being, the terrible loneliness of individualism. To love has to do with understanding what it is to be "one." Ceasing to be "I," centered on myself and that I live only for me, in order to bind myself into a true "us."

Among the glorious things that God allowed me to experience during the time of my tribulation, was one night in which Jesus revealed Himself in an unusual way.

I was falling asleep as I was worshipping in my bed, when I heard His voice say to me, "Come!" At that moment, my spirit found itself in the same place to which we had descended some time before, that dark place with the neon sign that said, "Direction Loneliness." But the place was lighter now, though always shadowy. It appeared to be an enormous, empty warehouse. It was about 165 to 195 feet in length. The walls were gray, and bare, except for the sign of "Direction Loneliness" that was hung high on one of the walls. The difference is that now it looked very small.

In the back of the room, almost out of sight, there was a chair with the figure of someone seated in it. I approached with care. I didn't know where I was, and the place was not at all appealing. As I got closer, I realized that the One seated there, with his head lowered and pensive, was Jesus. He was extremely sad. I was afraid to interrupt His silence. I just watched Him, until He raised His face and looked at me. I will never forget that look; the pain that was in it pierced my heart.

Then I dared to speak, and I asked him, "Why are You here? Why are You so sad? What is this place? Where are we?"

He took a few seconds before answering, and then He said, "This is the place of my loneliness, the place where my beloved NEVER COMES."

It broke my heart upon realizing the terrible selfishness that still abounds in us. I didn't know what to do. I only said, "No, Jesus, never again. At least I will come. I want to love you in all of your ways, even in the ones where the pain is unbearable."

"If you want to know love," He said, "there are paths of deep pain that you will have to walk at My side, but you will see the fruit of your affliction, and you will be satisfied."

Within The Depths Of God's Heart

Unity and love are life. The life of God, manifested in its true way, necessarily seeks to unite and to love. He loves to the end, until He bleeds to death in the greatest pain, as in the case when one that He loves, chooses eternal separation from Him.

This is the greatest pain in the heart of God, the deep hollow of emptiness and rending, of knowing that He will never again be with those that chose, by their works, hell. Love cannot stop loving. And, eternally, He will continue loving and mourning them. When God permits you to live in your own heart what He feels, when you can touch for just a second the open wounds of His heart, all of your being breaks, due to this acute, insufferable pain. There is no imagination that can conceive it, or words to describe it. It is too terrible. And when you truly understand this, you will do anything, even putting your life on the line, so no one is lost.

This is the last and the most fervent prayer of Jesus. It is a cry from the depths of His being, because He understands the pain of separation. Jesus was with the Father when both loved and rejoiced in the splendor of wonderful love between Themselves and the first couple. Jesus was with the Father when the devil and sin removed, suddenly, and by the roots, the one that They had made, "Their beloved."

I can hear in my spirit, and I can almost not continue writing, the singular shout of pain that was heard throughout the universe, when the heart of God was pierced by the mortal knife wound of sin. From one instant to another, the one who was the apple of His eye, His delight, His fullness of joy, the one into which He emptied Himself and she into Him, suddenly had been violently pulled from His arms.

I can perceive the deep silence in the heavens. Her voice will no longer be heard in the garden. His voice will no longer find echo in a heart in love and thirsty for His love. In a part of Himself, God was alone.

His beloved had surrendered to death. Day and night for centuries, the devil would butcher her, humiliate her. He would take pleasure in taking her to the most extreme reaches of the cruelest and unmerciful pain, and, all of this, before the very eyes of her beloved.

The angels witnessed in silence, time and again the shivers of pain that shook the universe. When the wind blew in the night's quiet, Hosea the prophet heard Him cry from heaven.

When Israel was a child, I loved him and out of Egypt I called my son.

But the more I called Israel, the further they went from me. They sacrificed to the Baals and they burned incense to images.

It was I who taught Ephraim to walk, taking them by the arms; but they did not realize it was I who healed them.

—*Hosea 11:1-3*
(New International Version)

How can I give you up, Ephraim? How can I hand you over, Israel? ...My heart is changed within me; all my compassion is aroused.

—*Hosea 11:8*
(New International Version)

It was from this same wound that Jesus would leave in order to come to look for the one that had been lost to Him, and return her to the Father. This is love: that He that loved us first, gave His Only Begotten Son, ...in order to be returned to eternal life.

A little piece of God, that is our spirit, continues existing in every man. A little piece of God in every human being is the seal of love that, in the depths of his being, cries out to be able to find again that love from which he came.

John saw his beloved's heart being pierced before his own eyes. He saw the wound opened with the spear. Jesus had told them, "He who has seen Me, has seen the Father." Every lash on the body of Jesus, every jeer, every blow, every torn and flogged part of His flesh, was indelibly marked in the heart of the Father. "The Father is in Me and I am in the Father," and this was truth in every cell of Jesus. This is being one.

In the middle of the darkness that covered the earth, they lowered the body of Jesus. I can see John, together with Joseph of Arimathaea, feel together with them when the nails were taken from His hands and His feet. John touched His still-warm wounds. He held His lifeless body in his arms. Only he and five others, just six people, were permitted to touch His wounds and to clean them with oil and perfume.

When I was on the Isle of Patmos, and the Lord submerged me for four whole days inside the heart of the Father, I saw a close relationship between pain and the fountain from which life flows.

During one of those days, the Spirit took me to a different place. It appeared like the interior of a heart, but it was not the beautiful heart of the Father. There were deep and very painful wounds, but they were different. Diverse thick, dark liquids oozed out of the wounds. Other liquids were yellow or green, and each one smelled worse than the other. It was a horrible disease.

I asked the Spirit where it was, and He said to me, "In your own heart. What you are seeing and smelling is the odor of bitterness, the stench of resentment, and the decay of the grudge. Look at that other one," He said. And I saw a

wound that oozed black pus. "That is self-pity and victim-
ization." I remained silent. I could only cry in repentance.

Then he carried me inside the heart of the Father again.
The pain was unbearable. There were millions of wounds,
full of innumerable cuts, of sin upon sin, that had never
healed. On top of a wound there was another one, and
many more that could not close. There were the slaps in
the face of the opinions of men, rising up insolently against
Him. The wounds were there of those that show contempt
for holy things they don't understand. They kicked Love,
they pulled His beard, they disfigured His face, they
skinned Him with the blows of the whip. Upon His open
wounds they put the weight of the cross, they pierced Him
with nails, they made fun of Him miserably, they vented
their wrath upon Him.

And we have done this with other human beings, where
love dwelt and to whom "Love" loved.

Sin is not a light thing with which we can continue
to live, as if nothing were happening. Our sins continue
piercing and cutting the heart of the Father.

My body cramped up upon seeing such suffering. I felt
terribly grieved by the part of my life that contributed to
wounding Him and that, many times, not wanting to, I
continue to do it. It was a horribly painful place, but there
was, at the same time, an inexplicable peace.

From every wound a fragrant, and very beautiful aroma
came forth. There was no bitterness, or grudge, or pus, or
anything worldly. Everything was clean, clear, and transparent. I spent entire hours simply loving Him in that place,
and still I continue doing it in my intimate times with Him.
Loving Him with all of my heart, in that same place where

our attitudes and high-mindedness have rejected Him, cause some of His wounds to close. Love heals wounds.

This is what John did at Golgotha, and what he continued to do for the rest of his life. John understood what it was to be one with Him in everything. John understood the power of loving Jesus in every human being. When you love in this way, the heavens open.

God reveals Himself to those who truly love Him. He is seeking worshippers in spirit and in truth. Jesus is not seeking people who speak in tongues, whose lives are trivial and without commitment. To worship Him is to love Him with all of our heart, with all of our strength, and with all of our being; and healing His wounds by loving one another.

While I was in that ecstasy inside the heart of God, something wonderful happened. I had given myself in a deep love, asking Him to use my life to heal His wounds, that he would take me to the world in order to restore His love upon the face of the earth. Suddenly, it was as if a door opened, or more like a crack or an enormous cardiac valve. From there shone a brilliant and blinding light, and, from the midst of the brilliance, the voice of the Father was heard that said, "This is the source of My love."

Then a vision within the vision appeared, as if there were a translucent movie inside the heart of God. I saw two men fighting. One of them was enflamed with rage, and he railed against the other one. At that moment, an invisible hand scratched one of the walls of God's heart, and made a painful wound. The angry man was thrown out, separated from God at a dizzying speed. I only watched and remained silent.

Suddenly, from inside of that wound that had been made, a powerful stream of shining light began to flow. It came from the source of love; and, like an enormous cord of light, reached the man who had sinned through wrath, and He began to bring him again towards Himself. Then the Father spoke again from the brilliance, and said, "I cannot stand to be separated from those I love. This is My mercy, that is part of My great love, that when you distance yourselves from Me, I pour Myself into you, in order to bring you back to Me."

"Look," He said, "and fill the earth with My love, and make disciples of My love. These are my true disciples, those that manifest My love among men, loving one another. They are going to humiliate you many times, and they are going to reject you due to this love. But be humble, and seek them again, as I also seek all of you without rest. My love is infinitely humble."

Place me like a seal over your heart, like a seal over your arm; for love is as strong as death, its jealousy unyielding as the grave. It burns like blazing fire, like a mighty flame.

Many waters cannot quench love; rivers cannot wash it away. If one were to give all the wealth of his house for love, it would be utterly scorned.

—*Song of Solomon 8:6-7*
(New International Version)

Jesus asked the Father, and this was His last prayer:

That they all may be one; as thou, Father, art in me, and I in thee, that they also may be one in us: THAT THE WORLD MAY BELIEVE THAT THOU HAST SENT ME.

—*John 17:21*

Jesus Comes For His Bride

The Bible closes its pages with Jesus making the greatest love call to His Church, the invitation to enter into a marriage relationship with Him.

He has revealed Himself through the ages as Savior, as Healer, as Provider, as Liberator, and so on, in so many ways. But His final manifestation is as "Groom."

God is preparing the wedding of the Lamb. And He Himself calls those who are invited to this great celebration as "blessed." Nevertheless, there is a greater blessing than this one, and it is that of being "the bride."

And the Spirit and the bride say, Come. And let him that heareth say, Come. And let him that is athirst come. And whosoever will, let him take the water of life freely.

—*Revelation 22:17*

There are those who are invited, and others who will get married.

In the body of Christ, there are different levels of relationship with the Lord. One level is that of a son. Sons seek God as Father. They want to sit in his affectionate presence, to feel His loving caresses, but above all, sons are interested in their inheritance. Those having this level of relationship, stroll through the world, feeling like the sons of the Great King. They seek favors of their Father; they know they are His chosen people and royal priesthood.

When a message is preached about the inheritance of the saints, or about possessing the earth, sons overflow with joy because they are sons and, as such, heirs.

Another level is the one of servant. Servants are humble, accommodating, faithful, and, in their heart, look forward to the day when they are to be given their rewards. They dream about the crown of righteousness, about the crown of life, about hearing one day the Father saying, "Well done, good and faithful servant; you have been faithful over a few things, I will make you ruler over many things." They like to have positions where they can influence many people. Many of them look forward to being found worthy of the fame that God grants. And even though these levels of relationship are wonderful, there is a level that is higher, and this is the one of the bride of the Lamb.

The apostles of Jesus followed Him for different reasons; some, because they were awestruck by the miracles; others, because they were seeking positions within the kingdom. "Who will You leave in charge when You leave?" they asked Him. But only one, John, followed Him as "His beloved disciple."

The one who is His "bride" is not seeking inheritance, or rewards, or position, or fame; she wants Him. She is deeply in love with Him, and will do whatever is necessary for her Beloved. She will go wherever He goes.

The one who is His bride, is united to the Spirit, and together they have a cry that does not leave them day or night. The only thing she wants is to be with Him, to look into His eyes, and to lose herself for entire hours in the freshness and the intensity of his gaze. Her shout and her cry is a continual, "Come!"

She gets up in the morning and cannot begin the day without feeling Him by Her side. Her first thoughts are of

Him and no one else but Him. Her heart bursts with love songs for her Beloved.

She is barely awake and is already bathed in His glorious presence. Her lips are full of His name: Jesus! Jesus! Jesus! There is so much fullness in this name that she cannot stop pronouncing it. It is ointment poured upon her entire being. It is the air that she breathes. It is the only drink that satisfies her.

Hearing His name, hearing it resound within her, while He showers her with well-being, and woos her with the kisses of His mouth, is her supreme delight.

His kisses are the breath of life that unite their two spirits. It is when words are insufficient, and the only thing they desire is to bond, one with another.

This is His cry:

That they all may be one; as thou, Father, art in me, and I in thee...

—*John 17:21a*

And her cry is:

Let him kiss me with the kisses of his mouth: for thy love is better than wine.

Draw me, we will run after thee: the king hath brought me into his chambers...

—*Song of Solomon 1:2 and 4a*

When He kisses her, her heart seems to burst with unspeakable joy; and her kiss floods the heavens with a delicious aroma.

On one occasion, while I was worshipping and I felt "those kisses of His mouth," the Lord took me in spirit to heaven. There, I saw Jesus seated on His throne and, around Him, the most magnificent celestial worship. There were myriad of angels, harmonizing beautiful songs, others flew around, making twirls and pirouettes in a dance full of harmony and perfection, while the glory radiated above the throne, making reflections of light that left one speechless.

I found myself close to the throne, at a distance in which I could easily see the face of Jesus. He was pleased with the worship, but His eyes denoted dissatisfaction. His presence was very reverential; it could not be interrupted by any circumstances. Therefore, I remained in silence, observing everything in detail.

Upon seeing His face, I felt very discouraged when I thought that if that worship did not satisfy Him, what hope did I have, that my little songs could please Him?

Suddenly something happened. The face of Jesus began to change and to become filled with a glorious light. He leaned over, barely remaining seated on the edge of the throne, as if something extremely important was about to occur. Then He raised both arms and signaled for all the angels to be silent. Instantly they were quiet. I hardly dared to even breathe.

Everything remained ecstatic, in a most solemn order. The angels that danced had moved to the sides, and before the throne, was a tiled floor of the deepest blue. From in the middle of the floor, a ribbon of smoke began to flow, that rose until touching the face of Jesus. He began to smell it, and the entire place was filled with an exquisite fragrance. While He enjoyed this strange perfume, His face filled with joy and radiated more intensely.

It was at that moment that He turned and looked towards where I was. His gaze found mine, and I felt that it pierced through me with a wonderful love. Then He said, "This is what fills my heart with fullness, the true and sincere worship of My beloved."

I returned from the vision, with a deep feeling of gratitude, to think that we, being nothing in comparison with what He is, fill Him with delight with our love and with our worship.

In the churches and in the conventions where God has taken me, I observe the people many times, when the time comes to worship. Sadly, the vast majority only sing in order to fill the moment, but their minds and their hearts are not with Him. But among them, there is a remnant, whose voice goes through the ceiling and arrives to the very heavens. It is the bride of the Lamb that is seeking that kiss, that union of substances in the depth of the spirit, that is where one touches and drinks of life.

"...He who thirsts, come." She is always thirsty for Him. The day that she does not see Him face to face, (because the beloved is permitted to see His face) or for some reason His voice was not heard, that day, she feels incomplete. The vital essence of her being has been absent and she goes out to seek Him with fervor.

She will stop at nothing. She will expose herself to danger if it is necessary, she will run day and night. She will shake the heavens with her cry. She will not quit. She has tasted the water of marital love, and she can no longer live without it.

I opened for my lover, but my lover had left; he was gone. My heart had gone out to him when he spoke. I looked for him but did not find him. I called him but he did not answer.

The watchmen found me as they made their rounds in the city. They beat me, they bruised me; they took away my cloak, those watchmen of the walls!

O daughters of Jerusalem, I charge you—if you find my lover, what will you tell him? Tell him that I am faint with love.

—*Song of Solomon 5:6-8*
(New International Version)

It is to the bride that the intimate secrets of the Groom are revealed. It is to her that He opens His heart to give her parts of Himself that He does not share with servants or with sons, but only with her.

There is a love that comes from God, that is not the love of the Father, or of the Friend, or of the Teacher. It is a passionate love. It is a love that is liquid fire that runs through your veins. It is a love that lights up the spirit and enfolds you in a brace that transports you to places in Him that are reserved only for the bride.

This love seeks total possession. It is not satisfied with fragments of love; it wants it all. It will do whatever is necessary to tear down every obstacle that gets between He and His beloved. As a turbulent river that no one can stop, He levels and knocks down, without mercy, everything that separates Him from His greatest love.

This kind of love, inevitably destructive, shatters the ego, love's mortal enemy. It will arise as a furious lion against strongholds of fear, with which men protect their own heart, in order to love with reservations.

He that feareth is not made perfect in love.

—*1 John 4:18b*

This kind of love does not allow a halfway commitment, or hearts that are cautious of giving themselves. It will break arrogance and self-sufficiency into fragments. It will demand your all, in order to pour itself into you. It will trample over common sense many times, putting to shame Phariseism and religious mind-sets.

This type of love does not respect formalisms, or structures of men. It is like Jesus as He was seen setting people free and healing them on the Sabbath, without worrying about the protocol of the law, because the essence of all law is love. And love comes before rules. It is the greatest of all of God's attributes. It is higher than justice and than wisdom, and than the law itself.

The marital love of God is like a consuming fire that will take you to places that will terrify you, where the limited soul of man fills with fear upon seeing the point to which the love of God is capable of giving itself. And it is then that He asks you the question, "Will you follow me wherever I go? Do you really love me in such a way, that you want to become one with everything that I am, and in the deepest levels of My love?"

"This is how I love," says the Lord. "Every day I put my open heart, without reservations, in the hands of every human being. And every single day, they tear it to pieces. And the following day, I do not give them less of Me, but I put it all again, exposed, without caution, without limit, in order for it to be destroyed again. And while they knife it day after day, in the heavens resounds My voice, "Father, forgive them, for they don't know what they are doing!"

Rational man is afraid of love, because loving costs everything, because love and pain are intrinsically connected.

The true bride of the Lamb will follow Him wherever He goes. She doesn't ask questions; she simply follows. She trusts wholly in Him, and even though He takes her to death itself, she continues trusting in Him. She knows Him intimately, deeply. And death for her is her final victory, that which will unite her intimately and forever with her beloved.

On one occasion in which the Lord was preparing my heart for the great trials that were approaching my life, He brought a dream that shook me to the most sensitive fibers of my heart.

I saw myself floating in outer space. Our planet appeared small in the distance. Then I saw an enormous silver pistol, with a short but very powerful barrel. At that moment, silver bullets began to go out from it, one after another, slowly approaching the earth.

As in a close-up of a camera, my spirit penetrated the atmosphere, until I could see in detail the people within a city. The gigantic bullets began to arrive, and everyone was running in every direction through the streets while they shouted again and again, "No, we don't want it!" The bullets then fell to earth and disintegrated.

Then I saw among the crazed multitude, some who had remained quiet, and, smiling, they extended their hands and waited for the bullets to fall upon them. When the bullets penetrated their bodies, the silver changed into light, and they were invaded by the indescribable splendor of God. Little by little, they began to transfigure until the only thing that was seen was the image of Jesus.

When I awoke from the dream, I asked the Lord, "What are these bullets?"

"It is My love," He answered me.

"Your Love? And why do You identify it with bullets?" I asked.

"Because this kind of love is a love that kills. To know the depths of My love is also to know the deepest dimensions of pain and to understand the price, and what it means and what it costs to truly love."

"Many want nothing more than My blessings, but they do not know Me, though they know about Me. To know Me means to penetrate, to understand, and to make yourself one with everything that I am."

"In these last days, I am choosing from among My people those who will be My bride. They are those who have been crucified to the world and all of its desires in order to follow Me. And I am going to transfigure Myself into them, and My glory will be seen in them, because I honor those who honor Me. And the world will know those who know Me and have seen Me, and who just talk about what they have heard, but they are more afraid of man than of Me."

And the Spirit and the bride say, Come. And let him that heareth say, Come. And let him that is athirst come. And whosoever will, let him take the water of life freely.

—*Revelation 22:17*

6

PENETRATING THE
INVISIBLE KINGDOM

God wants to take us to glorious dimensions in this new 21st century. He wants to allow us to understand and to experience things that eye has not seen, nor ear heard, neither has entered into the heart of man, but that God has prepared for those that love Him, and that he is already granting to those who will reign with Him.

The Lord wants us to understand that He has made His invisible kingdom accessible to us through Jesus Christ, His Son, that we can see it, hear it, feel it, and even penetrate it and move within it.

Jesus came to this world with three main objectives:

1. To save the world from sin
2. To destroy the works of the devil

3.   To bring the kingdom of God among us
      He himself said, casting out a demon.

If I with the finger of God cast out devils, no doubt
the kingdom of God is come upon you.

—*Luke 11:20*

He came in order to be the path that unites two worlds,
two kingdoms, two different dimensions: the spiritual
kingdom and the material kingdom.

I ask you to open your spirit as you read these lines, since
the principles that I am about to present to you are key in
order to enter in to possess the greatest spiritual riches that
you have ever experienced.

Ephesians 1:9 says:

Having made known unto us the mystery of his
will, according to his good pleasure which he hath
purposed in himself:

That in the dispensation of the fullness of times he
might GATHER TOGETHER IN ONE ALL
THINGS IN CHRIST, BOTH WHICH ARE IN
HEAVEN, AND WHICH ARE ON EARTH;
EVEN IN HIM.

—*Ephesians 1:9-10*

This is the glorious principle that we have begun to
discover in this book. In Jesus, the two realms are united,
in Him the heavens are a visible, palpable reality, as well as
the earth. In Jesus, there is no limitation in passing from
one side to the other, in moving in one dimension or in the
other. He said, "Whatever I see the Father do, I do. Everything I hear the Father say, I say."

And this is our great inheritance, being able to enjoy both realms, being able to penetrate them, experience them, live in them, and cause the truths of that invisible kingdom to pass from one dimension to the other.

Jesus came to the world in order to manifest the kingdom of God. Jesus did not come to the world to give us sermons on behavior, or to tell us a bunch of rules about what we should and should not do. That was already written in the law. Jesus came to return to us that which was lost: the kingdom of heaven, visible on the earth.

Jesus, upon coming in the flesh, made possible that the heavens and the earth became one, and that these two realms became palpable through two different kinds of eyes, the natural eyes and the eyes of spiritual understanding.

What man lost in the Garden Of Eden, was having within himself the same image of God. God made man after His image and His likeness, and this does not refer to our external form or to the inward qualities of our soul. The image of God in Adam was what permitted him to see God openly. God and man were one, because they were from the same image. The clothing of the glory of God covered him and, because of that, he did not feel naked. The two dimensions were visible at the same time. This is the image of God.

It is Jesus' will that we can see, feel, and move in these two dimensions. For this to happen, it is necessary for our spirit to be set free from the thick veil of unbelief and darkness that shadow our minds and hinder us from being what God has purposed us to be, a limitless Church, according to the image of the One who created us.

Paul, who understood these two dimensions perhaps better than any other apostle, wrote in the second epistle to the Corinthians:

> But their minds were blinded: for until this day remaineth the same veil untaken away in the reading of the old testament; which veil is done away in Christ.
>
> But even unto this day, when Moses is read, the veil is upon their heart.
>
> Nevertheless when it shall turn to the Lord, the veil shall be taken away.
>
> —*2 Corinthians 3:14-16*

I want you to notice here that the Word talks about a blinding of the mind and a veiling of the heart that must be removed.

Now, I want to take you to a deeper level than that of salvation. Here, you must understand that this conversion that the apostle is talking about is not referring only to the moment of accepting Jesus as Lord and Savior, but to the genuine conversion of the heart that makes us enter into supernatural dimensions of the kingdom of God.

The vast majority of Christians today have a lot of difficulty believing that God desires for them to be able to move in an impressive, supernatural power. And it is even harder for them to believe in the possibility of seeing the heavens open and the glory of God manifesting itself.

Nevertheless, the scripture continues in Corinthians, saying:

Now the Lord is that Spirit: and where the Spirit of
the Lord is, there is liberty.

—*2 Corinthians 3:17*

This verse of scripture, normally used to justify speaking
in tongues, dancing, clapping, or any manifestation of
external expression, is not referring to these things. What
the Holy Spirit wrote through Paul, talking about the true
liberty of the Spirit is the following:

But we all, with OPEN FACE BEHOLDING as in a
glass the glory of the Lord, are changed into the same
image from glory to glory, even as by the Spirit of the
Lord.

—*2 Corinthians 3:18*

Wow! What Paul is saying is that upon tearing the veil
that dulls our understanding, we can see with open face
everything that has to do with the kingdom of God.

Now when the Holy Spirit uses the word "beholding",
it does not mean feeling goose bumps, or quivers, it means:
TO SEE.

This is the promise of the liberty of the Spirit for us, that
everything that dulls our mind, the veil of darkness and
spiritual limitation, is torn by the Spirit, and this takes us to
a face to face encounter with the glory of God.

The real prison is found in the mind, full of corruption,
of unbelief, and of human structures of understanding, that
has been blinded by the devil. What we need to be set free
from, is ourselves, set free from our logical, limited ways of
seeing and doing things.

In whom the god of this world hath blinded the minds of them which believe not, lest the light of the GLORIOUS GOSPEL OF CHRIST, WHO IS THE IMAGE OF GOD, should shine unto them.

—*2 Corinthians 4:4*

Unbelievers are not only those who have not come to salvation, but also those who, due to their unbelief, cannot enter into the supernatural dimensions of the kingdom of God. Unbelievers are those who live a mental Gospel, but who have not understood what it truly means to enter and to possess the kingdom of God. And, I dare to say, that there are millions of people who are saved, but who have never entered in to possess everything that the kingdom of God provides for us. They believe that they will enter when they die and go to heaven, but this is not what Jesus came to teach. He said, "The kingdom of God has come upon you."

The design of God in order to transform us into His image, is not through a thousand sermons, or five hundred books by wonderful authors, but rather through being with him, beholding Him "with open face."

Christianity today, unfortunately, in most cases, is made up of people more or less instructed and informed, but who have not been converted to the dimensions of His glory, in order to be transformed into the image of God.

Jesus came to restore that which was lost. And what was lost mainly was the image of God in man. God created us in His image and in His likeness. This does not mean our physical image or our mental and psychic qualities. It is much deeper than that.

As I mentioned before, the image of God was what gave Adam and his wife the ability to look at Him with open face in the freshness of the afternoon in paradise. It was what gave them intimate and real communion with Him. It was what made them a bidimensional being (one that is in two dimensions at the same time).

Jesus, made flesh, is the image of God in this earthly plane, and Jesus simultaneously moved in the spiritual world and in the natural world.

It is in conforming ourselves again to His image, that which will allow us to move in all of the power of the kingdom of God. It is having His image again that which opens the celestial doors in order to receive the most remarkable revelations of His glory.

The scripture says,

> The first man is of the earth, earthy (referring to the fallen nature of Adam): the second man is the Lord from heaven.
>
> As is the earthy, such are they also that are earthy: AND AS IS THE HEAVENLY, SUCH ARE THEY ALSO THAT ARE HEAVENLY.
>
> And as we have borne the image of the earthy, WE SHALL ALSO BEAR THE IMAGE OF THE HEAVENLY.
>
> —*1 Corinthians 15:47-49*

The Lord wants us to have His image once again, while we are here on the earth, and, the way in which He designed this wonderful transformation is through a living, real encounter with the glory of God.

When you are looking at that glory, when you spend hours looking at it with open face, your spirit begins to impregnate itself with everything that He is. It is a real experience that affects your entire being.

When you look at Him, your level of faith arrives at stratospheric heights, everything becomes possible, feasible.

The real prison in which we find ourselves is in our own mind, full of unbelief and veils that hinder us from seeing. But, glory to God, who provided for us the Spirit, so that, wherever He is, our spirit is set free, and we can enter into dimensions and extraordinary levels. This is what it means to be able to see the Kingdom of God.

> For God, who commanded the light to shine out of darkness, hath shined in our hearts, to give the light of the knowledge of the glory of God in the face of Jesus Christ.
>
> *—2 Corinthians 4:6*

You can almost hear Paul groan in the epistle to the Ephesians, when he says, full of the fire of God:

> Cease not to give thanks for you, making mention of you in my prayers;

> That the God of our Lord Jesus Christ, the Father of glory, may give unto you the spirit of wisdom and revelation in the knowledge of him:

> THE EYES OF YOUR UNDERSTANDING BEING ENLIGHTENED; that ye may know what is the hope of his calling, and what the riches of the glory of his inheritance in the saints,

And what is the exceeding greatness of his power to us-ward who believe, according to the working of his mighty power,

Which he wrought in Christ, when he raised him from the dead, and set him at his own right hand in the heavenly places.

—Ephesians 1:16-20

The true encounter with the liberty of the Spirit will enable you to see the kingdom of God and its glory.

The cry of the Spirit is to see a transformed Church, moving in the same power as Jesus Christ, and doing greater works than the ones that He did when He was on the earth, as He Himself declared.

Can you really see God and live? Of course! This is the glorious experience reserved for all those who truly love Jesus. Jesus said,

Yet a little while, and the world seeth me no more; BUT YE SEE ME: because I live, ye shall live also.

—John 14:19

He taught, saying,

Blessed are the pure in heart: FOR THEY SHALL SEE GOD.

—Matthew 5:8

Follow peace with all men, and holiness, without which no man shall see the Lord.

—Hebrews 12:14

Also while praying to the Father, He said:

Father, I will that they also, whom thou hast given me,
be with me where I am; that THEY MAY BEHOLD
MY GLORY, which thou hast given me...

—*John 17:24*

When the mantle and the prophetic anointing manifested
themselves in the Old and in the New Testaments, the
servants of God saw the glory in many ways. The Spirit
of prophecy is the testimony, the revealed truth of all that
Jesus is.

Daniel saw the Ancient of Days, seated on His throne
of fire (Dan. 7). Ezekiel saw the expanse of His glory and
the cherubim around the throne (Eze. 1). Jacob saw the
heavens open and angels going up and down (Gen. 28).
Moses spoke with God face to face, as one talks with one's
friend (Ex. 33:11) Gideon saw the Angel of the Lord, who
was none other than Jesus, before His parousia in the flesh
(Jdg. 6). Likewise, Joshua saw Him in the form of a man
with a sword (Jos. 5:13). Paul was taken to the third heaven,
where he saw unspeakable things (2 Cor. 12:2). John was
taken to heaven innumerable times in order to see the entire
Revelation. And the examples are numerous of the reality
of the two dimensions, coming together and men entering
and experiencing the kingdom of God.

This will not happen in your life overnight. It takes time
and dedication. You need to train your mind to quiet itself
in order to be able to hear the Spirit. It is necessary to learn
that in the silences with the Lord, something wonderful
begins to happen. It is in this search that God begins to
manifest Himself, that the soul, subject to the Spirit, begins
to decrease and to change or, that is to say, to become

transformed into the likeness of the Lord. It is there, in that moment that the veils tear apart and the first experience begins.

First, it will be a delicate radiance or a strong presence of His Spirit. Then, it will continue to grow, and the radiance will become clearer and sharper, until you begin to see His face.

This is not imagining His face; this is receiving His image in your spirit. His image is not like the pictures from the Renaissance. God is multifaceted (He has many forms). Each manifestation of His attributes, of His power, or of His Name itself, changes the configuration of His image. And it is precisely this, which breaks the molds, and you begin to know Him truly, as a Person.

This is the promise of God for your life, and you have to appropriate it for yourself, no matter what the cost, because it is truly the pearl of great price. He said it and He will do it.

...Where the Spirit of the Lord is, there is liberty.

> But we all, with open face beholding as in a glass the glory of the Lord, are changed into the same image from glory to glory, even as by the Spirit of the Lord.
> —2 Corinthians 3:17b-18

Jesus Came To Manifest The Kingdom Of God

We are talking about extraordinary things, perhaps very new for many, because it is necessary for us to understand that we are entering into the most glorious era in history.

All things are being shaken, transformed, because it is written:

> And he shall send Jesus Christ, which before was preached unto you:

> Whom the heaven must receive until the times of restitution of all things, which God hath spoken by the mouth of all his holy prophets since the world began.
>
> *—Acts 3:20-21*

The Spirit Himself declares to us:

> Whose voice then shook the earth: but now he hath promised, saying, Yet once more I shake not the earth only, but also heaven.

> And this word, Yet once more, signifieth the removing of those things that are shaken, as of things that are made, that those things which cannot be shaken may remain.

> Wherefore we receiving a kingdom which cannot be moved, let us have grace, whereby we may serve God acceptably with reverence and godly fear.
>
> *—Hebrews 12:26-28*

(Jesus didn't come to give us moral teachings, or to emphasize the law. Jesus came to bring us the kingdom of God. He came to bear witness of that kingdom. He came to manifest, with His own life, all that the Father is. The most impressive thing about His ministry was not what He said, but the supernatural nature of His deeds.)

If I do not the works of my Father, believe me not.

But if I do, though ye believe not me, believe the works: that ye may know, and believe, that the Father is in me, and I in him.

—John 10:37-38

Jesus wanted to show us everything that happens when the kingdom of God manifests itself. Why did Jesus walk on the water? Did it make sense? Did He perhaps want to make sure preachers would have a pretty passage so that they could preach about how you can walk above the circumstances? No! He wanted to manifest the kingdom. He wanted to tell us, "If you move in My kingdom, this is a spiritual dimension that even dominates all matter. My kingdom is more powerful than all created things. It dominates everything."

He asked Peter, "Do you want to try it? Come, you can walk, too! What I am coming to bring you and teach you is for you, too. Get out of the boat, Peter!" (Paraphrased) And Peter, grabbed on to the faith that the kingdom produces, entered that dimension and began to walk upon the water.

When Jesus' mother, upset because the wine had run out at the wedding of Cana, asked Him to do something, He did not get up, filled with faith that he could collect a powerful offering and send for wine. He preferred to manifest His kingdom. "Fill the waterpots with water." And then He said, "Draw out now, and take it to the governor of the feast." (John 2:7-8)

When He was in front of the multitude that did not have anything to eat, and His disciples asked Him, "Master, do you want us to buy food and give them something to eat?"

He said, "No." Obviously, they had money in order to buy the food, otherwise, they would not have asked that question. But Jesus wanted to manifest the creative power of His Father. He wanted to manifest the kingdom. He asked them what they had. And they said just two fish and five loaves of bread.

Jesus took them in His hands. And what He did was to introduce them, submerge them, in the dimension of the kingdom, the realm of the Spirit. At that moment, the bread and the fish stopped being only a part of the natural realm. The kingdom began to impregnate them. Heaven and earth were united in that food. The multiplying, creative power of the kingdom took control over every particle of matter.

In the kingdom, everything can be multiplied. Everything can be created or restored. Then He said, "Pass them out." And at His order, the bread and the fish multiplied by thousands.

This is what is happening to those who are being submerged in His kingdom. This is what needs to happen to you, and you will see the most extraordinary things begin to happen.

The most important thing for Jesus was manifesting the kingdom, that they could see the Father through Him.

He said to Phillip:

If ye had known me, ye should have known my Father also: and from henceforth ye know him, and have seen him...

Jesus saith unto him, Have I been so long time with you, and yet hast thou not known me, Philip? He that hath seen me hath seen the Father; and how sayest thou then, Show us the Father?

Believest thou not that I am in the Father, and the Father in me? The words that I speak unto you I speak not of myself: but the Father that dwelleth in me, he doeth the works.

—*John 14:7, 9, 10*

Oh! If we all could really understand this; Jesus, made flesh, the Father doing the works in Him. This is what He is trying to say: the kingdom of God is among us; the heavens and the earth, united in Jesus.

That is the promise for our time: a kingdom generation that will impact the whole earth, not a handful of healing and miracle ministries that we can count on our fingers, but an entire generation, bringing the heavens down.

The kingdom has the power to establish all of the designs of God upon the earth. It is the kingdom that activates the will of God in the heavens, and then His will descends and manifests itself upon the earth.

When the disciples saw the greatness of the works that Jesus did, they realized that the Teacher worked in such a way that the heavens manifested themselves. Then, they said to Him, "Lord, teach us to pray." And He gave them the key in order to bring the power of God upon the earth.

But thou, when thou prayest, enter into thy closet, and when thou hast shut thy door, pray to thy Father which is in secret; and thy Father which seeth in secret shall reward thee openly.

—*Matthew 6:6*

After this manner therefore pray ye: Our Father which art in heaven, Hallowed be thy name.

THY KINGDOM COME. Thy will be done IN EARTH, AS IT IS IN HEAVEN.

—*Matthew 6:9-10*

The prayer of Jesus had its focus, first of all, in exalting the Father, and then, the most important thing, was that for which He had come: that the kingdom be established and that the heavens and the earth be made one.

Entering into the kingdom is the key to knowing Him, and it is also the key to power. Jesus did not say, "Go, preach salvation only." He said:

And as ye go, preach, saying, The kingdom of heaven is at hand.

Heal the sick, cleanse the lepers, raise the dead, cast out devils: freely ye have received, freely give.

—*Matthew 10:7, 8*

The training that Jesus gave to His disciples and the command with which he sent them was to manifest the kingdom.

...As my Father hath sent me, even so send I you.

—*John 20:21b*

In other words, as I came to be a witness of My Father, to show you His power and His greatness, so you too have to testify about the kingdom, to be living messages, where the kingdom is so entrenched within you, that everything you do and say manifests it.

He also said,

> And this gospel of the kingdom shall be preached in all the world for a witness unto all nations; and then shall the end come.
>
> —*Matthew 24:14*

To preach the kingdom of heaven is not a message in order to convince someone, in order for them to be convinced in their intellect, but far from a genuine conversion. Rather, it is to produce works that will bring, as a result, authentic conversions.

Paul confronts the Church, saying:

> But I will come to you shortly, if the Lord will, and will know, not the speech of them which are puffed up, but the power.
>
> For the kingdom of God is not in word, but in power.
>
> —*1 Corinthians 4:19, 20*

Today, this is practically never taught as a part of evangelism training, in the vast majority of churches. They teach a whole series of convincing, verbal techniques, that assist the unbeliever accept a momentary prayer and, in some cases, be attracted to a local church.

In many cases, we have filled churches with people, but we have not filled them with sons, converts to the kingdom.

God wants sons who possess the kingdom, and He is raising a generation that understands all this, a generation of brave people, bold and holy. Men and women who know how to pray in order to bring the kingdom to earth, a people who penetrate the kingdom, at all costs.

And from the days of John the Baptist until now the kingdom of heaven suffereth violence, and the violent take it by force.

—Matthew 11:12

7

The Entrance To The Kingdom Of God

I s Everyone Who Says They Are Born of God, Truly Born Again?

Nicodemus, that important man among the Jews, who came to Jesus by night, was a man instructed in the scripture, fearful of God, and who believed that Jesus Christ came from God. What he did not know was how to enter the Kingdom of God. Jesus told him:

> ...Verily, verily, I say unto thee, Except a man be born again, he cannot see the kingdom of God.

> Nicodemus saith unto him, How can a man be born when he is old? Can he enter the second time into his mother's womb, and be born?

Jesus answered, Verily, verily, I say unto thee, Except a man be born of water and of the Spirit, he cannot ENTER into the kingdom of God.

—*John 3:3b-5*

I want you to read this passage, going beyond the message of salvation with which we are so familiar. God wants to give us something immensely powerful for this century, which will cause us to enter into the true dimension of power and of revelation that is our heritage. I dare to say, and I do not feel that I am wrong, that this passage is much deeper and worthy of repeated study than the simple announcement of the Gospel that leads us to receive Jesus as Lord and Savior and to assure ourselves of eternal life in heaven.

Here Jesus is talking about seeing the kingdom and entering into the kingdom.

I believe that when Jesus truly enters into the heart of man to live, his spirit is sealed for salvation, and it is also awakened to begin to understand spiritual truths and to be able to feel the manifestations of the Spirit.

Nevertheless, as I have traveled to the different nations of the world and have talked with thousands of Christians and pastors, I realize the tragic reality. The vast majority of the people of God have never seen the kingdom of God, have never had a face to face encounter with Jesus, have never seen the heavenly places in which they have so often been told they are seated. And the most terrible thing is that the vast majority of them have never been born again.

Notice what Jesus says next:

That which is born of the flesh is flesh; and that which is born of the Spirit is spirit.

Marvel not that I said unto thee, Ye must be born again.

The wind bloweth where it listeth, and thou hearest the sound thereof, but canst not tell whence it cometh, and whither it goeth: so is every one that is born of the Spirit.

Nicodemus answered and said unto him, How can these things be?

Jesus answered and said unto him, Art thou a master of Israel, and knowest not these things?

Verily, verily, I say unto thee, We speak that we do know, and testify that we have seen; and ye receive not our witness.

—John 3:6-11

Here Jesus wants us to understand what is the true design of a son of God born of His Spirit: it is a person who can see the invisible dimensions of the kingdom. How is this possible? We said in past chapters that he who comes to Jesus is one spirit with Him. Now, I ask you, what are the chances of a spirit that has become one with God not being able to see, hear, and feel the Spirit of the Lord? The answer is absolutely NONE!

I will go even further: if the heavens and the earth are united in Jesus and Jesus is one with us, then what possibility is there that a born-again believer would not be able to see the kingdom of heaven? The answer is also none.

We just read that Jesus said to Nicodemus that unless someone is born again, they couldn't see the kingdom of God. Again I emphasize that to see means to look at with our spiritual eyes. Jesus could testify about the kingdom because he saw it.

> ... But what he (Jesus) seeth the Father do: for what things soever he doeth, these also doeth the Son likewise.
>
> —*John 5:19*

> ... We speak that we do know, and testify that we have seen...
>
> —*John 3:11*

Then where is the error? Why then can't millions of Christians that we call "born again" see the kingdom of God? Why can't they hear the voice of God? Obviously, the problem is not in the passage of Nicodemus. The problem is, rather, in the way in which we have understood it and preached it.

At some point in history, it occurred to someone to begin to preach that at the moment that a person said the sinner's prayer in order to receive Jesus as their Lord and Savior, they were born again. Somehow this became common knowledge. When we brought someone to the feet of Jesus, we prayed for him, and then we gave him a hug, saying, "Now you are born again." This became so normal that Christians began to be called "born-again Christians." In this manner, every person who became a part of the congregation automatically was called "a born-again believer."

Let's analyze this in depth. God is a God of designs. Everything that He created is made according to a divine model. All things were created from the invisible to the visible. This means, not that they were created from nothing, but that they were first conceived in the spiritual world and then brought to the visible, natural world.

In none of the designs of God, in heaven or earth, do we see that when a seed is planted, the plant is born instantly. We do not see any design in which an embryo is conceived in the womb, in an animal or a woman, and at that moment, the baby is suddenly born.

The supposed instant birth, in my opinion, is not a design of God. His model is as follows: sow the seed, water it, allow the seed to split inside the earth, and then it will root itself, and, in time, the plant will come forth. The same thing occurs in the womb: the seed is sown, there is a time of gestation, and then the womb opens, and the child is born.

When John speaks to us about being made sons of God, he says,

> But as many as received him, to them gave he power to become the sons of God, even to them that believe on his name:
>
> Which were born, not of blood, nor of the will of the flesh, nor of the will of man, but of God.
>
> —*John 1:12-13*

This word "born" is the Greek word gennao, that means to conceive in the womb. This is the beginning of the process, not the birth. There is a big difference between being conceived and being born. When a child is in the womb of his mother, the parents already talk about him as their heir, but he can't enter into the possession of anything if he has not been born.

Jesus speaks clearly with Nicodemus and he gives him the characteristics of those who have really passed the period of gestation and have been born again. He says that these see the Kingdom, they have entered the Kingdom, and also, they are like the wind, that you can listen to and hear the sound of it, but cannot tell where it is coming from. So is everyone that is born of the Spirit (John 3:8, paraphrased).

> The wind bloweth where it listeth, and thou hearest the sound thereof, but canst not tell whence it cometh, and whither it goeth: so is every one that is born of the Spirit.
>
> —*John 3:8*

Here we see that Jesus is teaching him how to know if someone has been born of God. In other words, he is telling him that they are people that see the kingdom of God and that are continually guided by the Spirit, because they hear His voice in dazzling clarity.

When someone is born into the natural world, there is evidence. The baby sees, hears, and moves with obvious clarity in his new world. While he still formed part of God, he could not know this world. He first had to be born as a material being.

The same thing happens when we are born into the spiritual world. There also has to be evidence, and the evidence is that, upon entering the spiritual world, we see it, we hear it, and we move in it.

When my spirit was truly born to the spiritual world, the invisible world became clearly visible. Notice what Paul says to the Romans:

> For they that are after the flesh do mind the things of the flesh; but they that are after the Spirit the things of the Spirit.
>
> For to be carnally minded is DEATH; but to be spiritually minded is life and peace.
>
> Because the carnal mind (the blinded, dulled mind that cannot see God) is enmity against God: for it is not subject to the law of God, neither indeed can be.
>
> So then they that are in the flesh cannot please God.
>
> But ye are not in the flesh, but in the Spirit, IF SO BE that the spirit of God dwell in you. Now if any man have not the Spirit of Christ, HE IS NONE OF HIS.
> —*Romans 8:5-9*

Notice here that he who truly has the Spirit of Christ, is going to be guided by the same Spirit, to live a spiritual life; and he could in no way feel satisfied living a fleshly life and thinking fleshly thoughts, because he knows that this is enmity with God.

To truly have the Spirit of Christ, will lead you to preach to the lost and it will lead you to have mercy on the poor. It will lead you to a life of prayer and of bounty with the Father. It is not possible for Christ live in someone and this person go one year or five years without preaching to someone, as is the case with the vast majority of people who fill our churches today.

For if ye live after the flesh, ye shall die: but if ye
through the Spirit do mortify the deeds of the body,
ye shall live.

For as many as ARE LED by the Spirit of God, they
are THE SONS OF GOD.

—*Romans 8:13-14*

Here we see that the seed that was produced upon
receiving Jesus in one's heart can die, or can be aborted, by
the death that is contained in carnality. We also see how in
the passage of Nicodemus, those born of God, the sons who
have entered into the manifestation of their birth, these are
led by God.

What does it mean to be led by the Spirit of God? This
is the internal voice that manifests from Spirit to spirit in
order to give direction to our steps.

It is the voice that Ananias heard when the Spirit told
him,

...Arise, and go into the street which is called Straight,
and inquire in the house of Judas for one called Saul,
of Tarsus: for, behold, he prayeth,

And hath seen in a vision a man named Ananias
coming in, and putting his hand on him, that he
might receive his sight.

—*Acts 9:11-12*

It is the angel, manifesting himself to Philip, and saying:

And the angel of the Lord spake unto Philip, saying,
Arise, and go toward the south unto the way that

goeth down from Jerusalem unto Gaza, which is desert.

—*Acts 8:26*

It is the voice of the angel that spoke to Cornelius and said:

And now send men to Joppa, and call for one Simon, whose surname is Peter:

He lodgeth with one Simon a tanner, whose house is by the seaside: he shall tell thee what thou oughtest to do.

—*Acts 10:5-6*

It is the angel that appears to Peter in jail and, touching him, said:

And the angel said unto him, Gird thyself, and bind on thy sandals. And so he did. And he saith unto him, Cast thy garment about thee, and follow me.

—*Acts 12:8*

Beloved reader, you can see the heavens and the earth united into one. The angels were manifesting themselves and interacting with the sons of God. This is our promise as sons of God.

We see how there can really be a difference between a born son, meaning "manifested" and a son not yet born, and, in the worst case scenario, someone in whom the seed could have died.

It is illogical to think that someone who says he has been born of the Spirit, has no evidence of knowing and moving in the spiritual world.

The Lord gave us a very clear example, explaining to His disciples about the kingdom of God. He compares it to a sower who goes out to sow:

The sower soweth the word.

And these are they by the way side, where the word is sown; but when they have heard, Satan cometh immediately, and taketh away the word that was sown in their hearts.

And these are they likewise which are sown on stony ground; who, when they have heard the word, immediately receive it with gladness;

And have no root in themselves, and so endure but for a time: afterward, when affliction or persecution ariseth for the word's sake, immediately they are offended.

And these are they which are sown among thorns; such as hear the word,

And the cares of this world, and the deceitfulness of riches, and the lusts of other things entering in, choke the word, and it becometh unfruitful.

And these are they which are sown on good ground; such as hear the word, and receive it, and bring forth fruit, some thirtyfold, some sixty, and some an hundred.

—Mark 4:14-20
(and Luke 8:15)

Here we see how the seed of Jesus, sown in the heart, only gives fruit in one fourth of those in which it is sown. The rest of the seeds died. They dried up due to a lack of water of life, they were drowned by pleasures, by desires, or by the greed of this world. Perhaps they call themselves living, but, in reality, they have already died, or are about to die.

The Apostle John gives us a clear diagnosis in order to recognize those who are born of God and those who just have the external form.

Before delving into this, I want you to feel with me what God feels for His Church, how much He loves her and wants to see her alive and full of power. That is why I am writing the way I am, not in order to condemn anyone, but so that we all enter into this new millennium possessing everything that He wants for us. God is literally shouting from the heavens: REFORMATION! A NEW REFORMATION IS NECESSARY. BEHOLD, I COME SOON!

When I began to hear this shout in the heavens, I stopped in order to seek His face and to understand what it was that He so desperately wanted to say. It was then that I began to understand and to realize the true condition of the present day Church. Why is so much power, so much anointing, so much promise of blessing preached, and the people of God remain as if they were tortured, trapped in innumerable failures, weak and full of sin and carnality?

God wants to raise His Church to immeasurable heights, but He can't do it until we realize our reality, until we speak the truth.

The Apostle John entered the third heaven many times! He knew the kingdom, saw the face of Jesus, and enjoyed experiencing it every day. He penetrated the infinite depths of love, and he knew God intimately and gloriously. And he is the one that said:

Whosoever abideth in him SINNETH NOT: whosoever sinneth HATH NOT SEEN HIM, NEITHER KNOWN HIM.

Little children, let no man DECEIVE you: he that doeth righteousness is righteous, even as he is righteous.

He that committeth sin IS OF THE DEVIL; for the devil sinneth from the beginning. For this purpose the Son of God was manifested, that he might destroy the works of the devil.

Whosoever is BORN OF GOD doth not commit sin; for his seed remaineth in him: and HE CANNOT SIN, BECAUSE HE IS BORN OF GOD.

—1 John 3:6-9

What does it mean that he cannot sin because the seed of God protects him? It means that the seed is very powerful, it is God Himself inside of our being. And what this produces is that when someone proposes sin to you, something stronger than you opposes it. Even though you would like to sin, there is a force inside of you that stops you and makes you take off running, as Joseph did when he was enticed by Potiphar's wife. It is a power that, when you are tempted, it will not allow you to sleep, it steals your peace, it shakes you, it does the unspeakable in order to keep you from sinning.

This does not mean that you will never fall; but if you were to slip, as soon as you touch the ground, you will come back shouting, seeking His mercy. He will not allow you to remain there even one day. The experience will be so strong that you will radically distance yourself from that seduction.

It is as when Peter sinned. It was an experience of true hell, knowing that he had failed the very one that he loved so much. And from there he rose up powerfully, to the point that he gave up his life for Him.

The seed simply cannot live together with sin.

For if ye live after the flesh, ye shall die...

—Romans 8:13a

John goes on to say:

In this the children of God are manifest, and the children of the devil: whosoever doeth not righteousness is NOT OF GOD, neither he that loveth not his brother.

—1 John 3:10

We know that we have passed from death unto life, BECAUSE WE LOVE THE BRETHREN. He that loveth not his brother ABIDETH IN DEATH.

Whosoever hateth his brother is a murderer: and ye know that no murderer hath eternal life abiding in him.

Iereby perceive we the love of God, because he laid down his life for us: AND WE OUGHT TO LAY DOWN OUR LIVES FOR THE BRETHREN.
—1 John 3:14-16

I believe that those who are born of God have a continual experience with the water of life. They are people whose spiritual levels begin to be felt and recognizable by the rest of the body. They are people who no longer belong to this world, but who have left the things of this world, and truly, irrefutably belong to the kingdom that is not of this dimension, the kingdom of God.

I believe that when Jesus talks about being born of water and the Spirit, He is not necessarily referring to baptism in water, but to waters of revelation, waters of life that flow from the very throne of God. Those who are born again are necessarily worshippers, tireless seekers of God, men and women God has brought to drink from these waters, and who know how to get to these waters and drink from them.

When the Bible speaks of water in this passage, it does not say baptism, as the Bible so clearly names it when referring to baptism in other parts of the Scriptures. Theologians have assumed that it is baptism, but here it says water, and there are many different kinds of water in the Word.

But whosoever drinketh of the water that I shall give him shall never thirst...
—John 4:14a

From your inner being will flow rivers of living water, and these are those whom I am seeking, the true worshippers in Spirit and in truth (paraphrase of John 4). I am not seeking those who sing songs, but those who know how to take their worship to the very presence of His throne room.)

The New Birth And Kingdom Levels

Upon submersing myself in depth in order to understand this reformation that God wants, I began to understand some things that, through listening to so many theologies, had previously just brought me confusion. Some theologies say that one can never lose one's salvation, while others affirm that it can definitely be lost. This matter has done nothing more than to create divisions.

Other powerful servants of God and I have arrived at the conclusion that there are different kingdom levels. Upon understanding it in this way, many pieces of the puzzle find their place.

First Level ● Study

This is the encounter with Jesus Christ, the level in which we are impregnated with the seed of life. We have the light of truth, and we know that Jesus is our only, all-encompassing Savior. This is the level that we will call "of John the Baptist." John recognizes the Savior, preaches and announces the Messiah, but he does not have the manifestation of power and miracles in his ministry. He has defeat in the midst of trials, as when he sent the message to ask Jesus if He was the one or should they wait for another.
The majority of God's people are at this level. They recognize their salvation, but they are children that have yet to learn how to be conquerors and enter into their Promised Land.

In this level we find the promise of the kingdom, but not its manifestation. If the person dies at this level, he enters in to possess the riches of the kingdom after his death.

In Galatians 4:1-7, Paul draws an analogy to this respect, using a context that was common to Jewish traditions. In Hebraic thought, a father has his offspring. They are his potential heirs, but they are not considered "heirs" until they reach the age of 30 and enter into what is called "the adoption as sons." At that moment, that father would choose from among his sons, as he thought best, not all of them, and would call them "heirs."

> Now I say, That the heir, as long as he is a child, differeth nothing from a servant, though he be lord of all;
>
> But is under tutors and governors until the time appointed of the father.
>
> Even so we, when we were children, were in bondage under the elements of the world:
>
> But when the fullness of the time was come, God sent forth his Son, made of a woman, made under the law,
>
> To redeem them that were under the law, that we might receive the adoption of sons.
>
> And because ye are sons, God hath sent forth the Spirit of his Son into your hearts, crying, Abba, Father.
>
> Wherefore thou art no more a servant, but a son; and if a son, then an heir of God through Christ.
>
> —*Galatians 4:1-7*

It is under this principle that Jesus has to wait to be 30 years old in order to enter in to possess His ministry. And when he entered the water, the Father from heaven said, "This is my beloved Son, in whom I am well pleased." Thus the acknowledgment that Jesus was "the inheriting Son" of the Father was fulfilled publicly.

This same analogy applies also to the Christian who is a child. He is a potential heir, but until he dies to the rudiments of the world, that is, to the principles by which this world conducts itself, he cannot enter in to possession of that which is rightly his.

This is the person who receives the seed of the kingdom, has been impregnated by God, and is in the process of being broken and of dying to this world in order to be born again. If he is able to overcome and die to the flesh, he will enter the second level of the kingdom.

> ...That we must through much tribulation enter into the kingdom of God.
>
> —*Acts 14:22b*

If he permits his spiritual life to die, due to his carnality, he will be aborted and he will not be born again.

Second Level

This is the spiritual adolescence and what we will call the level "of Jesus in His ministry, before the resurrection."

In this stage, he already has been born again, and we see the clear manifestation of a signs and wonders ministry. Authority is seen in the believer and he has a growing, healthy spiritual life. In this kingdom level, the devil already begins suffering defeats through the active diligence of the warriors of God. The believer is ordained in the ministry, and people follow him because they see the favor of God upon his life. He clearly hears the voice of God and is definitely guided by the Spirit. However, he still does not have all authority.

Third Level

This is spiritual maturity and which we will call the level "of resurrected Christ." Here we already enter into much more advanced kingdom levels. Here the devil has been already totally defeated, and the believer enjoys "all authority." In this level the active union of all things is seen, those that are in heaven, as well as those that are on the earth (according to Ephesians 1:9).

This is the authority of the resurrection. This is that which Paul cried out for with all of his strength, paying the price of terrible chains and the highest levels of inner death.

> That I may know him, and the power of his resurrection...
>
> —*Philippians 3:10a*

And he continues, saying:

> Not as though I had already attained, either were already perfect: but I follow after, if that I may apprehend that for which also I am apprehended of Christ Jesus.
>
> —*Philippians 3:12*

We have been apprehended for a kingdom without limits, where heaven and earth are bonded together, becoming one. At this level, Jesus is now a conqueror, the firstborn, with all authority. He can go to heaven and return, as when he appeared to Mary Magdalene and said:

> ...Touch me not; for I am not yet ascended to my Father: but go to my brethren, and say unto them, I ascend unto my Father, and your Father; and to my God, and your God.
>
> —*John 20:17*

He is also seen to appear among His disciples and then disappear.

> Then the same day at evening, being the first day of the week, when the doors were shut where the disciples were assembled for fear of the Jews, came Jesus and stood in the midst, and saith unto them, Peace be unto you.
>
> —*John 20:19*

Here Jesus is going to introduce new and deep levels of the kingdom.

> To whom also he showed himself alive after his passion by many infallible proofs, being seen of them forty days, and speaking of the things pertaining to the kingdom of God.
>
> —*Acts 1:3*

It is at this level that we are going to see the most extraordinary spiritual battles against the high ranks of the forces of darkness, the fulfillment of the possession of Jesus Christ's total and absolute victory.

And the kingdom and dominion, and the greatness of the kingdom under the whole heaven, shall be given to the people of the saints of the most High, whose kingdom is an everlasting kingdom, and all dominions shall serve and obey him.

—Daniel 7:27

It is at this level in which heaven and earth are united, where I see the fulfillment of Hebrews 6:4-5:

For it is impossible for those who were once enlightened, and have tasted of the heavenly gift, and were made partakers of the Holy Ghost,

And have tasted the good word of God, and THE POWERS OF THE WORLD TO COME,

—Hebrews 6:4-5

Fourth Level Study

This is the level of the total invasion of heaven upon the earth, which we will call the level "of Christ ascended to heaven and seated on the throne."

It is the level of the glory of God filling all the earth, of the total restoration of all things, the level where the tabernacle of worship is manifested upon the earth.

It is the level of total government of the celestial over the earthly. I believe that very few will reach this level. These are those who will govern with Christ and to whom He will give authority to judge.

And I saw thrones, and they sat upon them, and judgment was given unto them...

—Revelation 20:4a

And he that overcometh, and keepeth my works unto the end, to him will I give power over the nations:

And he shall rule them with a rod of iron; as the vessels of a potter shall they be broken to shivers: even as I received of my Father.

—*Revelation 2:26-27*

Now, coming back to the matter of the new birth in relationship to the four kingdom levels. The big problem comes when I read, first the parable of the sower, where definitely I see that only one fourth of the seed was that which came forth out of the ground and produced fruit. That is why I believe that only one fourth of those that have been impregnated with the seed of salvation really obtained it, and the other three fourths, for the different reasons Jesus mentioned, were aborted and need to be re-impregnated or else they will not enter eternal life. However, I also believe that Jesus will do the unspeakable in order that none will be lost.

He said clearly:

Not every one that saith unto me, Lord, Lord, shall enter into the kingdom of heaven; but he that doeth the will of my Father which is in heaven.

—*Matthew 7:21*

This brings to mind another great dilemma of Scripture, which we find in Hebrews 6:4-6:

For IT IS IMPOSSIBLE for those who were once enlightened, and have tasted of the heavenly gift, and were made partakers of the Holy Ghost,

And have tasted the good word of God, and the powers of the world to come,

IF THEY SHALL FALL AWAY, TO RENEW THEM AGAIN UNTO REPENTANCE; seeing they crucify to themselves the Son of God afresh, and put him to an open shame.

Study To understand   —*Hebrews 6:4-6*

(My question is how many Christians claim to have the Holy Spirit, speak in tongues, and are sinful, fallen or have returned to the world? The answer, beloved reader, is millions. How many pastors and servants have fallen, about some of whom it is known to be so and of others it remains hidden? Thousands. If it is impossible for them to be renewed unto repentance, then they are condemned, and there is no hope for them. But, knowing the infinite love of God for us, the answer is obviously another one.

I believe the answer is found in making ourselves conscious of the different kingdom levels. I think and believe that this comes from God: that in the first two kingdom levels, the seed can be aborted, but that it can also be re-planted through sincere repentance. And it is because of that that we see people who have left the Gospel and later returned, who were restored. What we have just read in the epistle to the Hebrews applies only to levels three and four (those who received power of the world to come).

I believe that it is also practically impossible for someone that God allows to arrive at these last two levels to return to sin.)

A Prayer For You

I want to take this moment to pray for you, beloved reader. Perhaps, through reading these words you have realized that your seed was suffocated by the cares of this world, by sin, or that the heat of intense trials dried its barely born spiritual life, or the devil stole it from you. The truth is that you do not feel the guidance of the Spirit in your daily life. You do not hear the voice of God. You do not perceive the spiritual world, or have evident manifestations of the presence of God in your life.

If this is you, allow me to pray that God would re-impregnate His Spirit in you. Pray this prayer with me:

Heavenly Father, I ask forgiveness for not having diligently taken care of the pearl of great price, that was Your very life in me. Forgive me, because the cares and the pleasures of this world took preeminence until I stopped feeling You. Today I want to return to you with all of my heart.

Take a few moments and look at the state of your soul before Jesus, nailed to the cross, dying for you. Ask the Holy Spirit to reveal the condition of your soul. See your thoughts, your motives. See the force behind what is truly deciding the course of your life. And see Jesus, carrying your sin in the most horrendous pain.

Do not continue reading until you can embrace Jesus crucified, and you can leave all of your sins in every one of his wounds. He suffered them due to His love for you, and this is not a light thing. This is the most important revelation in order to begin a victorious life with Him.

Now, ask Him, with your own words, to sow His Spirit in you, that He help you walk in uprightness and in holiness, and that, this time, you will take care of that seed until it bears fruit, thirty, sixty and one hundred fold.

And I proclaim upon His life, that from today forward, you enter into the kingdom of God as a new creature, impregnated by the Spirit, and that all of the designs that the Lord has for your life will come to pass. That from today forward, you will be a victorious Christian who reaches the highest levels of His kingdom.

8

REFORMATION...BEHOLD, I COME!

Since entering the 21st century, God showed me radical changes that will come upon the earth and upon the Church. I remember that I was worshipping at a convention at the end of 1999, when I saw the heavens open and an enormous book descend, as large as the size of a city.

In its open pages, I saw thousands of men and women with authority. When they spoke, all submitted to them, because they were men of great renown. They were ministers of God. Their voices were eloquent, but they turned their backs on one another.

Then I heard the voice of God that said, "This is the Book of Life in which are written all of my designs." At that moment, a gigantic page began to lift up, and it turned over in order to fall upon the previous page. The Lord spoke again, "I am turning the page of history. The

Church of the 20th century has been left behind, and those who remain bound to its structures will be silenced. Many of the influential voices that you have heard until now, you will no longer hear. I am raising up a new generation that will fear me, and will speak what I give them to speak. It will not speak on its own, but I will tell it what to speak. It will be a generation that will love me and will honor me, because it will have more fear of me than of men."

As I listened to the Lord, the page was slowly falling. As the space between the previous pages and this one grew narrower, the voices were being silenced. They shouted desperately in order to be heard, but no more sound came out of their throats. The page finished falling, and there was a brief silence. Then I saw on the new side of the page, a series of new, fresh people, full of the presence and the glory of God, and their voices began to make incredible sounds. I saw many young people, some middle-aged men and women, and very few old men.

Jesus is coming soon, and He is coming for a glorious Church that will manifest Him upon the face of the earth.

God is coming with great power upon His people in order to shake everything that needs to be shaken, so that the immovable remains. And He will use the base and the despised of the world in order to put the wise to shame. A clear difference will be seen between the people of the kingdom and the religious people of the Church. And a wave of His irresistible power, of His love, and of His glory will cover the earth as the waters cover the sea.

1. A Glorious Gospel Will Be Preached

But if our gospel be hid, it is hid to them that are lost:

In whom the god of this world hath blinded the minds of them which believe not, lest THE LIGHT OF THE GLORIOUS GOSPEL of Christ, who is the image of God, should shine unto them.

—2 Corinthians 4:3-4

I can hardly sleep, hearing the Holy Spirit groaning day after day for the Church. He loves her so. He regrets seeing her in the fire, as He saw her when she was conceived in the heart of the Trinity. Before the world was, He already saw and rejoiced about all of the glorious plans that the Father had for His beloved.

Rejoicing in the habitable part of his earth; and my delights were with the sons of men.

—Proverbs 8:31

Jesus came to preach a glorious Gospel, a Gospel that transforms and changes lives, a Gospel that is the news of His great power and of His Kingdom coming among us.

Jesus spent forty days after His resurrection, teaching His disciples the mysteries of the kingdom, giving them the keys in order to train a powerful Church, a Church where signs, wonders, and revelation would make the glory of God visible.

They did not have Bibles or books published by great Christian authors, but they had the Holy Spirit. They depended on Him for everything. What occurred when they received the Holy Spirit was so impressive that the Word says:

> And when they had prayed, the place was shaken where they were assembled together; and they were all filled with the Holy Ghost, and they spake the word of God with boldness.
>
> —*Acts 4:31*

They did not need training courses or Sunday schools in order to go out and do the work of God. Now, I am not against this. But I want us to realize that they saw something. They were exposed to something that was so genuine, so true, so full of power, that it converted them into instant ministers.

When we are full of the Holy Spirit, a glorious Gospel comes out of our lips that transforms the soul.

When I was converted in 1985, I saw the power of God in an extraordinary way in the psychiatric hospital where I was confined. I was full of the Holy Spirit. And, in the fifteen days that followed my conversion, the psychiatric hospital was practically emptied, as I was casting out demons and healing the sick. I simply believed. As it is written:

> And these signs shall follow them that believe; In my name shall they cast out devils; they shall speak with new tongues;

They shall take up serpents; and if they drink any deadly thing, it shall not hurt them; they shall lay hands on the sick, and they shall recover.

—*Mark 16:17-18*

Today I do not see that this is the experience of thousands and thousands that attend our churches every day. Somehow the Church of the 20th century, that had many bull's eyes and moments of great revivals, healings, and wonders, also committed grave errors.

I want you to look at a reality together with me, because the desire of my heart is not to criticize anyone. What I want is to bring a little light, so that together we can make a diagnosis of what is good and of what is bad. In this way, we will be able to help the Church grow healthy and powerful, which is the desire of Jesus.

Today in the vast majority of churches, and in the lives of the people in particular, we find congregations in which all of the work is done by perhaps 10% of the church, while the other 90% warm the pews. The church lives defeated, complaining about everything, talking bad about everybody. They are physically and emotionally sick, and a large number of them have serious financial problems. They live a carnal life, without power. Sinning is not an important issue for them, but they do want all of the blessings of God.

Every time a powerful man or woman of God comes, they run to the altars to receive the anointing. But after receiving tons of anointings, they go on the same, and they don't do anything with that which was imparted to them.

The other 10% carry on as best they can, with a tremendous workload, both inside and outside of the church. They are exploited in a miserable way by the people, who are not concerned with even their most basic needs, but who demand everything from them. They live on their knees, crying to God to move the congregation forward and pay the bills. Meanwhile a large part only give God the minimum and rob Him of their tithes and offerings.

The pastors live, carrying a burden that is killing them, without the people having the slightest pity for them. They are overwhelmed and abused by the hundreds and thousands of people that are only seeking their own wellbeing and answers for themselves. The burden and the responsibility become so strong that if a sheep changes churches, it becomes a motive for division between some pastors. Fear begins to invade decisions, because the stress level becomes so high. The love and liberty that should reign are exchanged for attitudes and spirits of control.

Many times when I enter to pray in the presence of God and He opens His heart to me, I can hear the deafening shouts of the pastors and the ministers of God, who simply cannot take it anymore. This is one of the most clamorous noises inside of the heart of God. The cry of the desperate, exhausted servants, who have no one to talk to, with whom they can pour out their soul, while the devil roars in their ears in order to eat them alive.

They must maintain the appearance of joy and wholeness, but inside they are bleeding to death. The rigid structure of the intolerant Church, without mercy, inhumane, holds them prisoners. They want to leave, but they don't know how.

I want you to know, beloved servant who is reading these lines, that God hears you, and you are not alone and that God is about to do something radical in order to help you. He loves you infinitely, and He knows what you have been going through. He has cried with you every time you have cried, every time they have persecuted and crucified you unjustly. And your reward in heaven is great.

I remember one time when Pastor Rafael Jimenez preached at a convention that we held for leaders in Mexico City. There were about 1,200 pastors in the auditorium of the hotel. Suddenly, the Spirit took him and, with a contrite heart, he said, "God is showing me that there is more than one pastor here that has said, 'If God doesn't do something, this very week, I am going to kill myself.'" There was a deadly silence in the room. Then he made an altar call in order to pray for them. You can't imagine my surprise to see that more than 400 pastors ran to answer that call. The cry of those pastors literally sent one's soul into spasms.

On another occasion, as I worshipped the Lord, God showed me in visions the Lord Jesus, galloping on a white horse. His face was furious, as I had never seen it before. Before Him was an enormous iron building, full of people who groaned. Then he stopped before it, and he took out an iron rod. And with only one movement of great force, he struck the metallic structure, and it unexpectedly fell to the ground. At that moment, He turned and looked at me and, with a great voice, he said, "Tell my people that I am coming with an iron rod against the structure of religious rigidity that subjugates my Church; and tell them, he who does not leave from there, will feel my iron rod, and tell them that they do not yet know what my iron rod is like."

Something is very wrong, and it is about to kill the spiritual life of very valuable people.

Where did we go wrong? Where did we begin to take a wrong turn? Why don't we see that powerful Church that we preach about so much?

Pastors, leaders, Church, it is necessary that we stop and bring radical change. Millions of people categorically can no longer continue living in a religious structure, in a structure of masks and without power.

What I see is that we have brought the people a diluted Gospel, a Gospel without commitment, a cheap Gospel. We have preached Christ as if he were the latest cookie on sale, that is your best option on the market, a Gospel made of rules established by good men and by men with a burden for the lost, but which has unfortunately omitted basic things.

In the vast majority of cases, repentance is never even preached to unbelievers. People are brought to the churches without ever having experienced a burden for their sins, without having ever even considered the state of their soul.

If salvation is by grace through faith, it also has a door. And that door is narrow, and the entrance is to confess our sins and nail our life with Christ on the cross of Calvary. This is the design of God in the tabernacle of Moses, where at its entrance the altar of sacrifice is found.

This is also God's model through Christ. He himself said:

...Except ye repent, ye shall all likewise perish.
—Luke 13:5

In the famous four laws to preach the Gospel that are taught today, one law is omitted that says it is necessary that you repent and give your life to Jesus. The consequence of having calls to salvation without sincere repentance and without a commitment by the new believer gives birth to churches full of sin and a lack of commitment.

A person who surrenders his life to Christ in the consciousness of a deep commitment, and being aware of his lost state, will receive salvation with deep gratitude and, as such, his walk will be one of surrender to God and faithfulness. This is not a personal opinion. This is a provable reality throughout the world.

Jesus did not give His disciples a little evangelistic sermon for them to learn by memory and then that they would take the message of salvation that they. He didn't tell them to hand out tracts either. (Obviously there were no printing presses.) But what I want to emphasize is that He did not give them the 20th century "evangelist's easy way."

Jesus sat down with them. He imparted to them the Spirit. He taught them how to cast out demons. He assisted them in discerning where sicknesses came from. He demonstrated the power, and He gave of grace freely so that they would, in turn, do the same. He spoke to them about the kingdom of heaven and the glorious possibilities that entering therein implied.

When He sent them, He said, "Preach, saying, 'The kingdom of heaven has drawn near to you." And then he instructed them to demonstrate what the kingdom is.

We get excited when we see hundreds of people in a stadium answer the call of salvation, and then we are surprised when not even 2% of them join a church. The problem is that there is something wrong in the way in which we invite people to come to Jesus.

full of the Holy Spirit, on the day of Pentecost, ...ed and 3,000 people were converted. He did not preach a pleasing little sermon that would not offend anyone. After demonstrating the power, he concluded saying:

> Therefore let all the house of Israel know assuredly, that God hath made that same Jesus, whom ye have crucified, both Lord and Christ.
>
> Now when they heard this, THEY WERE PRICKED IN THEIR HEART, and said unto Peter and to the rest of the apostles, Men and brethren, what shall we do?
>
> Then Peter said unto them, REPENT, and be baptized every one of you in the name of Jesus Christ for the remission of sins, and ye shall receive the gift of the Holy Ghost.
>
> For the promise is unto you, and to your children, and to all that are afar off, even as many as the Lord our God shall call.
>
> —*Acts 2:36-39*

— Powerful

Believe me, since those of us who have understood the glorious Gospel are experiencing it, thousands are coming to the feet of Christ and are entering the kingdom of God.

One day the Lord asked me a question, and he told me: "Ask this question to my people. What is the difference between inviting Jesus to be the Lord of your kingdom, and you entering the kingdom of God?"

The vast majority of Christians invite Jesus to be Lord of their kingdoms, but have never entered into His kingdom. And, what is worse, in many of them, He is not even their

Lord; He is their servant. The relationship they have with Him is not one of honoring the Lord, but one of "Give me! Help me! Provide for me! Heal me! Open the door! Close the door!" etc.

My prayer is: Reform, oh God, the preaching of the Gospel, so millions will know you and truly enter Your kingdom!

2. We Are The Temple Of The Living God

The design of God for our lives is that we truly be the temple of God upon the earth, His dwelling place. He does not want us to just have a divine touch, or simply a visitation. He wants to have His place of permanency in the life of each believer.

John finds himself in the middle of the vision of Revelation when he receives a measuring stick.

> And there was given me a reed like unto a rod: and the angel stood, saying, Rise, and measure the temple of God, and the altar, and them that worship therein.
>
> —*Revelation 11:1*

God wants us to understand something of fundamental importance here. Measuring has to do with height, with different levels, with different grades of revelation. It has to do with setting boundaries between that which is consecrated to Him and what cannot be touched by the enemy.

He shows something similar to Ezekiel, too. God desires to reveal to us his most sacred structures, and He wants us to conform to them so that He can set up His permanent dwelling in the temple of our spirit.

Thou son of man, show the house to the house of Israel, that they may be ashamed of their iniquities: AND LET THEM MEASURE THE PATTERN.

And if they be ashamed of all that they have done, show them the form of the house, and the fashion thereof, and the goings out thereof, and the comings in thereof, and all the forms thereof, and all the ordinances thereof, and all the forms thereof, and all the laws thereof: and write it in their sight, that they may keep the whole form thereof, and all the ordinances thereof, and do them.

This is the law of the house; Upon the top of the mountain the whole limit thereof round about shall be most holy. Behold, this is the law of the house.

—Ezekiel 43:10-12

When the Scripture speaks to us about the dwelling of God in man, it does it in an exclusive context: to those who love Him and keep His commandments, and not to everyone who calls Him, "Lord, Lord!"

The fact of receiving Jesus as Lord and Savior establishes us in a covenant of salvation, and it gives us a measure of the gift of God. The fact that He sets up His dwelling in someone is something deeper. He said:

At that day ye shall know that I am in my Father, and ye in me, and I in you.

He that hath my commandments, and keepeth them, he it is that loveth me: and he that loveth me shall be loved of my Father, and I will love him, and will manifest myself to him.

Judas saith unto him, not Iscariot, Lord, how is it that thou wilt manifest thyself unto us, and not unto the world?

Jesus answered and said unto him, If a man love me, he will keep my words: and my Father will love him, and we will come unto him, and MAKE OUR ABODE WITH HIM.

—John 14:20-23

Notice that the dwelling is not established until love and obedience to the Word are proven. He will come to dwell where He finds a Holy Temple, according to the designs of His house.

The angel tells John to measure three things: the temple, the altar, and those who worship at it. These are the three ingredients that God needs to find in us, in order to come and live there.

The principle that the temple of God must be built in us is very important, since God will not establish His dwelling if there is no temple or if there are only ruins.

When God told Moses that he wanted to make His dwelling among His people, first He revealed to him what the temple was like. Then He ordered that the tabernacle be sanctified, and then He descended in His glory to inhabit it.

The Lord speaks to Haggai to this respect, and, in our day, it is interpreted in a spiritual sense toward the Church, which is the Israel of the Spirit. And it says:

"Is it a time for you yourselves to be living in your paneled houses, while this house remains a ruin?"

—Haggai 1:4

Now, we do not think, as we have done for so long, that we see the building of the church as the temple of God. This is an abomination, since God does not dwell in temples made with hands. It does not refer to our physical houses either.

What the Lord wants to tell us is that our houses are paneled with all of the blessings that He had sent upon us, our talents, the riches of wisdom, our prosperity, health and so many gifts that we have received from Him. But His house, the one that is on His holy mountain in heavenly places, that house at which one can only arrive in true worship, with hunger and thirst of finding Him, that one is in ruins. That one is built, worshipping in Spirit and in truth. Unfortunately, we have so little understanding of what it means to really worship.

The Church has tried to sing beautifully, wanting to minister to Him. But, if we analyze what we call worship, in large part they are soft, beautiful songs, whose objective is not to render worship to God for His greatness. Rather their objective is that to touch us, fill us, change our heart, submerge us in His river, refresh us, etc., that would make us feel good.

Subtly our soul is pleased, while we change true worship for petitional songs, centered upon ourselves. In a service, perhaps six or seven songs are sung directed towards ourselves for every one of true worship to Him.

Something is wrong. Don't you think? Worship and the reason we come together must be Him. When we sing to Him, our spirit is raised with Him. When we sing in the direction of ourselves, the soul is the one that is raised. This is extremely subtle, because apparently everything feels very spiritual, but the fruit is going to be anemic and fleshly. God is going to attract millions of people to the place where He is being raised up.

A new move of worship is flowing upon the earth, directed towards glorifying the greatness and majesty of God. The songs of this new generation will exalt all of the attributes of God, and this will make His anointing, His presence, and His manifestation descend in a wonderful way. The spirit of the believers will be awakened and raised to new levels of experience with God and power.

When we worship in Spirit and in truth, we penetrate the realm of His glory, the heavens open, and we can look at Him with open face. And then we are transformed into His image.

Worshipping is not singing. It is literally converting yourself into the altar from which the river of God flows. It is not something that one can do. It is something into which you must transform yourself.

An angel took the prophet Ezekiel to experience the levels of this river. He first put him in up to his ankles, then up to his knees, and later up to his waist, until the river became so large that it could only be crossed swimming.

When the water is up to your knees, the flesh still controls, it decides. But when the river grows, it takes you wherever it wants to take you. They are no longer songs written by a songwriter (up to your knees). It is the flow from the very heavens, singing through your lips. It is a gush of water that makes robust trees grow on your right hand and on your left. It is a flow so powerful that it floods the spiritual realm and touches cities and even nations.

Oh, how He is seeking worshippers who worship Him that way!

Those who are His temple have understood that to worship is not a moment during the Sunday service, but a way of life, an intimate communion, a bonding themselves with God and God with them.

To worship is to become one with Him. It is intimate communion that quiets the soul until only the Spirit is heard. It is where the true union between heaven and earth is produced. The two realms begin to conjugate, and it is then that Christ is revealed.

Worshipping opens the prophetic dimensions so that you can see Him with open face, in order to see His glory, in order to see the most wonderful angelic manifestations, and that, under uncovered heaven, we can have extraordinary, spiritual experiences.

God is not seeking Sunday morning singers who speak in tongues, but a united people in intimate communion with Him, people who are the temple and the very song of God, instruments of God in the hands of the Spirit that He can play.

Oh, what a wonderful experience, to know that we were created for the praise of His glory, that within each one of us there are an innumerable quantity of instruments that He can play as He pleases. And when He does it, heavenly music flows from our mouths. It is not necessary to know how to sing or to take classes at the conservatory. When you become His instrument, the heavens themselves manifest. And, if you know how to sing, even better, but if not, God is made perfect in our weakness.

3. A Transforming Experience

A great truth about this is that we are transformed by what we worship. In Psalm 115, where God recriminates the worship of idols, it says:

> They have mouths, but they speak not: eyes have they, but they see not:
>
> They have ears, but they hear not: noses have they, but they smell not:
>
> They have hands, but they handle not: feet have they, but they walk not: neither speak they through their throat.
>
> They that make them are LIKE UNTO THEM; so is every one that trusteth in them.
>
> —*Psalms 115:5-8*

I remember one time I cried to God so that he would give me His creative power. I was convinced that it was His will to teach us how to make things descend from the invisible to the visible. I went to a retreat alone to the mountains of Costa Rica. And God said to me, "Worship Me as Creator!"

First, He confronted me with the twisted view I had of some of the creatures of His creation. At that time, I was terrified of fat, black, and hairy moths. And it just so happened that I was eating dinner and, beside the table, there was an enormous window. As I was eating, a black moth arrived and rested outside of the window at the height of my eyes. I stared at it with terrible disgust, and I said within myself, "How ugly you are! You couldn't be more horrible!"

At that moment, I heard the nearly audible voice of God that said to me, in a scolding tone, "Everything that I created is good, wise, beautiful, and I love it! Who are you to say that what I made is ugly? Perhaps you do things better than I? Didn't I put wisdom and camouflage into the wings of the moths so that they could defend themselves in that way from their predators? Isn't it wise that I put fat in their bodies so that they would have energy to fly at night? Isn't it wise and perfect all that I did? I made the night and its inhabitants, and I called them good, and I think they are beautiful. Everything that I created is good! I am the Lord of the day and Lord of the night. You are repulsed because men have covered with curse my nocturnal animals, my cave animals and my birds of prey. I made them with my wisdom and they groan to see the glorious manifestation of My sons, who are to set them free with My power."

I felt the pain of the Father. I had humiliated Him for years as Creator, and now I sought His creative power. I wept for a long time, for my arrogance and stupidity. And I asked His forgiveness. And I began to worship Him as Creator, as wise and perfect Creator.

Upon returning to San Jose, the capital of Costa Rica, I had to preach at a conference with my pastor, Rony Chaves. I asked God to manifest His creative power at that convention.

While we worshipped in one of the sessions set apart just for women, I saw in the heavens two thick, rough stones of gold and diamonds that floated over us. The Lord said, "Prophesy that they come from the spiritual to the natural." And I did it. Suddenly, numerous women began to run to the platform with diamonds in their hands that had formed supernaturally in front of them. We were full of joy. One woman, every time she closed her hand and opened it again, a new diamond was formed.

That night was also incredible, as during the entire service the people came and put jewels of gold in my hands as an offering. They put so much gold into my hands that there was enough to share with the rest of the preachers. Hallelujah!

To worship in Spirit and in truth, in the language of the Spirit, and in new song, brings the manifestations of God. This is the most important part of a service and the part that the vast majority of churches and conventions eliminate. It is in these moments when He speaks, when he changes hearts, when experiences and healings come.

He is seeking true worshippers, who will worship Him in Spirit and in truth. And this is going to make a great difference.

4. If I Am Father, Where Is My Honor?

One of the things that will be radically transformed in the Church of the 21st century is the concept of the offering.

The excesses with regard to the offering became abominable in the last decades. At one extreme, is the miserable way in which people think that they can approach God, giving Him their leftovers and robbing Him of their tithes. And, at the other extreme, is the prosperity movement in which some preachers missed the mark, completely giving an erroneous focus as far as the essence or the heart of giving offerings is concerned.

The principles are correct: give and you will receive. The same as: God multiplies the goods of the joyful giver, and that God wants us to prosper in all things.

The problem is the spirit behind the principle. When a person gives only with the objective of being prospered, he has lost the essence of giving offerings.

Giving offerings is an act of honoring God. It is the moment of the service in which we come to God to give Him honor as Father and as King. The vast majority of times that God speaks of being honored in the Bible, it has to do with the offering.

You can praise someone and, nevertheless, not honor him. He says in the book of Malachi:

> A son honoureth his father, and a servant his master: if then I be a father, where is mine honour? And if I be a master, where is my fear?...
>
> And if ye offer the blind for sacrifice, is it not evil? And if ye offer the lame and sick, is it not evil? Offer it now unto thy governor; will he be pleased with thee, or accept thy person? saith the LORD of hosts.
>
> Ye said also, Behold, what a weariness is it! And ye have snuffed at it, saith the LORD of hosts...
>
> —*Malachi 1:6a, 8, 13a*

God has been immensely despised and offended in this aspect of the offering, because the people are so centered on the offering itself, that they believe it is truly a pain in the neck. Or it falls into the other extreme and converts itself into a matter of financial investment, pushing aside the honor and solemnity due to the Father.

The offering is indeed a way in which God blesses us economically, but it was not designed so that the focal point would be us, but Him.

God gives us the privilege of being able to honor Him. And this is a very important way in which we minister to Him. This has to be a sublime moment. It is not about passing the offering plate to collect the money and doing it however it occurs to you, as a necessary, but bothersome part of the service.

No! God says, "I will honor those who honor Me and those who despise Me will be held in low esteem."

The offering is saying to God with our goods how much we appreciate Him, how much we honor and acknowledge Him as the most important Being in our lives, that He will receive the best of us.

To give offerings is a form of worship in which we are recognizing Him, giving Him our lives.

Money, in one way or another represents life. It is the produce of hours of work, of struggle. It symbolizes ideals, things that we desire, wellbeing, etc. But it is also the parameter that God uses to measure to whom He will surrender true riches and to whom he will not.

He says in His Word:

> He that is faithful in that which is least is faithful also in much: and he that is unjust in the least is unjust also in much.

> If therefore ye have not been faithful in the unrighteous mammon, who will commit to your trust the true riches?

> And if ye have not been faithful in that which is another man's, who shall give you that which is your own?

No servant can serve two masters: for either he will
HATE the one, and LOVE the other; or else he will
HOLD TO THE ONE, and DESPISE the other...

—*Luke 16:10-13a*

God wants to give us inconceivable things from His
spiritual and material riches, as well as from His power and
His wisdom. The one that understands what it is to love
God, gives everything without reserve; he gives Him his
life and, with it, everything that he possesses. These are the
ones that God will honor, giving them His Kingdom, His
honor, and His riches.

But here Jesus mentions another master, the one named
"Mammon." He is the god of the riches of this world. Jesus
calls him master, or boss, because a master is someone who
is obeyed and served.

Mammon has a kingdom and a terribly strong structure with which he dominates the kingdoms of the earth
and a vast majority of Christians. This spirit governs in a
subtle way and is very difficult to detect by the people of
God. Unfortunately, being ignorant of his devices is one of
the principle causes that impede us from possessing what is
ours.

His purpose is to be master, even of the saints of the
Most High, so that he can control our lives and Jesus will
be hated and despised. Can Jesus be hated and despised by
a Christian? Absolutely. This is what the Lord says we do
when we submit to the orders of Mammon.

One day, the Holy Spirit revealed to me how this demon
acted. He told me, "Mammon has a voice, and he talks to
his people, saying:

I am your master. I control your finances, your emotions. I am the one who tells you what you can do and what you can't do. I determine where you can travel and if you can travel. I decide where you buy your clothes, and what restaurants you can go to and which ones you can't. I am the one that says how you can treat the servants of God and what I do not allow you to do for them. I am the ones that decides how much you can give for an offering and how much you can't, and if I want to, if you tithe or not. I decide what school your children go to, and to which hospital you can take your family. Remember, I am the one that makes your budget, and I determine what you can do and what you can't, because I am your master. When you have to make a decision, I am the first voice you hear.

I torment you with anguish whenever I want. I have the power to use your temperament in order to also afflict your spouse, and I enjoy seeing how you submit to me. I love how you obey me when I tell you, "You can't pay for that trip to go to the Christian conference." Or when I tell you to be dishonest and you sneak into the event. I love it when you rob God. That is why I control your offerings, so He can never have control and I can continue telling you what you can and can't do.

I am the one that puts loathing in your heart about offerings. I want you to continue hating Jesus and obeying me. Remember I am your master, and you obey me.

This monologue of the devil can be as extensive and chilling as you want. But immediately it reveals clearly that Jesus is not Lord over a majority that sing hallelujah and that tell Jesus that they love Him, but their heart is governed by Mammon.

Jesus was so set against this spirit that He put a thief as treasurer. Why? He wanted to tell him, "My Kingdom is not ruled by money, but by my Father's power. If I have a need, I catch a fish with gold in its belly. If the people are hungry, I multiply food. If the wine runs out, I turn water into the best wine. Money does not decide what I can or cannot do, but my Father in heaven."

Jesus received many offerings, because the PURPOSE OF THE OFFERING IS TO HONOR GOD, NOT TO SUSTAIN THE KINGDOM. The kingdom of God and its work sustain themselves with the supernatural power of God. The power produces and attracts riches.

God can use money for His work or not. The solutions and the ways in which the kingdom operates are not necessarily going to require finances. Many offerings lack the supernatural power that they should have to bring blessing because they are taken in order to cover expenses.

The offering of God has never had as its design covering expenses. It was always to honor the Most High, and when He is worshipped in this way, He takes care of meeting the budget.

Occasionally we see voluntary offerings in the Old Testament in order to raise funds to build the tabernacle or the temple. But these were never the "command from the altar" that is the principle of presenting ourselves before

God, honoring Him. They are extra gifts that God certainly blessed, like were the alms of the saints for the poor.

The Lord is very pleased with a cheerful giver, one who gives things away freely, the altruistic giver, and these givers will certainly walk in the great blessings of God.

My focus in these lines, however, is that the lost honor of the offering return to its proper place.

9

THE GOVERNING CHURCH
OF THE 21ST CENTURY

As we saw in the previous chapter, God is calling the Church to govern the earth. The establishment of the kingdom of God implies one government that will replace another government, that is, the devil's.

John, while he received Revelation, saw a sign in the heavens:

> And there appeared a great wonder in heaven; a woman clothed with the sun, and the moon under her feet, and upon her head a crown of twelve stars:
>
> And she being with child cried, travailing in birth, and pained to be delivered.

And there appeared another wonder in heaven; and behold a great red dragon, having seven heads and ten horns, and seven crowns upon his heads.

And his tail drew the third part of the stars of heaven, and did cast them to the earth: and the dragon stood before the woman which was ready to be delivered, for to devour her child as soon as it was born.

And she brought forth a man child, who was to rule all nations with a rod of iron: and her child was caught up unto God, and to his throne.

—*Revelation 12:1-5*

Upon reading this passage, I can see the Church of the 21st century, a body of believers in which the glory of Jehovah shines. This is a Church of prayer, that groans and cries out in order to give birth to a generation that will govern the nations with a rod of iron. This Church understands that intercession must be made to the end, that is willing to suffer the pain and suffering of Christ until the sons of God are manifest in brilliance.

Paul said:

My little children, of whom I travail in birth again until Christ be formed in you.

—*Galatians 4:19*

It is a conquering Church, that will enter the breach and will fight awesome battles against the devil in order to give birth to the true kingdom of God on the earth. She has the heart of God. She wants to give birth to the plans and designs of God, and does not settle for less.

It is a Church of sleepless nights and fastings, a true mother who is concerned about her son who is about to be born. It is an apostolic and prophetic Church, where the heart of the fathers is for their children, and the heart of the children is for their fathers.

She is about to give birth to what the devil hates most. This man child is the one who will subjugate his entire empire, because he is seated on the throne of God.

Who is this son, so desired by the woman? It is the Church of the 21st century, the sons of the kingdom, the strong people that Joel saw, who have never been and will never again be in any other generation. These are a people of the fire of God, who cannot be defeated, who, even if they were to fall upon a sword, it would not harm them, the squadron of God that carves out and devastates the territories of the devil. Before her, Eden raises up, where heaven and earth are made one. No one escapes from her hand, because she governs and is victorious.

They are the radiant people that Isaiah saw, upon whom the glory of God rests, and kings walk in the brightness of their light, whose resplendence attracts everything toward itself, because God Himself is seen in them, and the riches of the world are brought to them (Isaiah 60, paraphrased).

Jesus speaks to John in different ways about this generation that precede His coming. He says:

And unto the angel of the church of the Laodiceans write...

—*Revelation 3:14*

In divine time, this represents the present day Church, the Church of the 20th century, upon entering the 21st century. It is a Church that feels that it has arrived at its finest hour, that has tremendous preachers. Its theology reaches incredible heights; its praise, too. Stadiums are filled, thousands of people are added to the ranks. This Church feels satisfied, and it says, "I have no need of anything."

Unfortunately, heaven does not see things the same as the earth does. And while we are dazzled by the huge crowds and man's show, from above, the perspective and point of view is quite different.

The Lord, watching from the heights, says, "From here, from on high, you look unfortunate, miserable, poor, blind, and naked. Your lukewarm attitude and your apathy make me nauseous. So I advise you to buy from me gold, refined in the fire, that you might be rich, and white clothing with which to dress yourself, that the shame of your nakedness would not be discovered, and anoint your eyes with eye salve so you might see.

I scold and chastise all those I love. Be then jealous and repent.

Behold, I am at the door and I am knocking; if anyone hears my voice and opens the door, I will enter into him and I will have dinner with him and he with me.

To him that conquers I will give allow him to sit with me on My throne, as I have conquered and I have sat down with My Father on His throne. (Revelation 3:17-21, paraphrased)

Here God is making a strong call, to an integral reformation. We have totally lost our way and the Church finds itself in a deplorable spiritual situation. Its lukewarm attitude, its apathy, its lack of integrity to walk in truth, makes the Lord want to vomit her from His mouth.

Nevertheless, it is from within this Church, disabled in His eyes, that God is calling this son who will govern with Him, that remnant of 7,000 (a figurative number) that Elijah saw who have not bowed their knees to the rudiments of this world.

We see this glorious trumpet blast in the final part of the passage where Jesus touches the door of our lives. This verse, that we use to bring the Gospel to the lost, has nothing to do with unbelievers, but with the Church of the end times.

Notice how, from the latter Church, conquerors arise that sit with Him on His throne:

...Her child was caught up unto God, and to his throne.

—Revelation 12:5

Here we see the open manifestation of the Kingdom upon this newborn generation. Everything begins with a sincere repentance of all of the areas of our indifference and spiritual lukewarmness. Then there is an intimate communion with Jesus. This dinner, mentioned in Revelation 3, is a covenant meal, an encounter of love, a date between spouses, of intimate friends. And then, He takes you by the hand and truly makes you enter into heavenly places.

The heavenly places are places that exist in the dimensions of His Kingdom, where one can enter, where God literally is drawing his bride to the third heaven, so that we can see, understand and enjoy His kingdom. Later I will talk about these heavenly places where already dozens of people are being taken. This is life in the kingdom. This is the inheritance of those that love Jesus. Today, I have already lost count of the times I have been taken to extraordinary places in celestial dimensions.

One thing is saying that we are seated in heavenly places with Christ, and another that you are categorically translated there, when He begins to shine upon you, and you feel His hand in yours, raising you up on high and seating you with Him upon His throne.

One thing is to fight battles, from below, proclaiming all of the verses that you know, and another is to fight from the throne of God.

This is what the devil is afraid of, that men and women would be seated with Jesus, upon the seat of His government. These are those who will conquer over all of the forces of evil and govern with Christ now and in His reign to come.

From the moment that this man child is raised for God, to govern from on high, a battle in the heavens is loosed in which Michael rises up to fight (Revelation 12).

This man child, this glorious Church, begins to see from God's perspective. It begins to have an understanding of the kingdom in a precise way, since it can see celestial dimensions with open face. This Church has taken position in the place of authority, where it cannot be conquered.

This is the same battle that Daniel saw, which looses times of great anguish that the earth will live, where the wise ones will shine as stars forever in eternity, and they will be times of great harvest (Daniel 12).

And in Revelation it says:

And there was war in heaven: Michael and his angels fought against the dragon; and the dragon fought and his angels,

And prevailed not; neither was their place found any more in heaven.

And the great dragon was cast out, that old serpent, called the Devil, and Satan, which deceiveth the whole world: he was cast out into the earth, and his angels were cast out with him.

And I heard a loud voice saying in heaven, NOW IS COME SALVATION, AND STRENGTH, AND THE KINGDOM OF OUR GOD, AND THE POWER OF HIS CHRIST: for the accuser of our brethren is cast down, which accused them before our God day and night.

—Revelation 12:7-10

Although the battle takes place in heaven, the saints on the earth, "the man child," are the ones that determine and are victorious, since it says:

And they overcame him by the blood of the Lamb, and by the word of their testimony; and they loved not their lives unto the death.

—Revelation 12:11

Notice that when the glorious Church, the man child, takes its position in heavenly places, sitting upon the throne, one begins to see salvation, true power, and authority on the earth. And it is when the kingdom of God is manifested upon the earth.

This generation of "the man child" conquers with the power of the blood. This is with a deep knowledge of the sacrifice of Christ. She has drunk of the blood of the Lamb. This means that she has bonded with the life, with the light that proceeds from the blood. She has drunk from all the love of total surrender contained in the blood, and for that reason, she loves in a way that cannot be overcome. She loves her neighbor to the very death. This is the greatest power in the universe, and love is the power that destroys the devil.

"The man child" conquers with the word of his testimony. This does not refer to the testimony of salvation, but to a life that literally testifies to the kingdom of God. Witnesses are those that bring evidence of what they have seen and heard of the glory of God. Their works and the presence of God in their lives bear witness that they are and they live in Christ and for Christ, and the Spirit moves with power in their lives.

Who Will They Be, This Man Child?

Now, how does God call and choose this generation?

We saw that he is knocking on the door of the heart of the apathetic, insensitive Church that is the present day Church and His instructions are in the book of Revelation, verses 17 to 20:

1. Buy From Me Gold Tried In The Fire

He says, buy from Me gold tried in the fire. When he says "buy," it implies a price to be paid. If salvation is free through faith, taking possession in places of government with Christ is not that way. Paul wrote:

If we suffer, we shall also reign with him...

—*2 Timothy 2:12a*

Gold refers to celestial wisdom, the comprehension of the kingdom, entering levels of fire that consume the veils that dull our understanding and that do not permit us to see with open face. Gold that is refined in the fire, is gold that spends a long time immersed in the intense heat that burns the dross.

One thing is to find ourselves with the fire of a ministerial call, with the burning bush of the presence of God, that takes us away from the priorities of the world and submerges us in the work of God, and another is to climb the mountain that burns with fire.

The first fire dazzles, attracts, and makes you fall prostrate and barefoot before His holiness. The second fire has the price of scaling the steep, smoking mountain with thunder and lightening. This is the mountain where the one arriving at its peak finds oneself with the designs that produce the glory of God to descend among the people.

This is the mountain where the darkness and tempest are felt, where one can no longer hear the voice of men, so only the voice of God is heard. To this fire, one must climb alone. To arrive, one must cross dense clouds, and feel as if everything were shaking under one's feet. It is when you enter the dimensions of God, that everything earthly is shaken and cracked to make you understand that there is nothing stable and eternal upon the earth.

But when you arrive up there, when you pay the price of finding yourself with the wisdom from on high, then you see Him with open face, His brilliant face over yours. You can never again return to earth, or appreciate the perishing things over which blind men fight in their covetousness. It is there that you hear Him say:

I love them that love me; and those that seek me early shall find me.

Riches and honour are with me; yea, durable riches and righteousness.

My fruit is better than gold, yea, than fine gold; and my revenue than choice silver.

I lead in the way of righteousness, in the midst of the paths of judgment:

That I may cause those that love me to inherit substance; and I will fill their treasures.

—*Proverbs 8:17-21*

2. Buy From Me White Raiment

Now that we are talking about a glorious calling to sit on the throne of God, I see that the clothes that are mentioned here are something much more powerful that the clothes of salvation.

We see the Church, the woman who gives birth to "the man child," cries out with labor pains, in the anguish of her enlightenment.

Paul also speaks about these clothes, which are not acquired simply by asking forgiveness of our sins, but they imply the whole process of giving birth. He writes:

For we know that if our earthly house of this tabernacle were dissolved, we have a building of God, an house not made with hands, eternal in the heavens.

For in this we groan, earnestly desiring to be clothed upon with our house which is from heaven:

If so be that being clothed we shall not be found naked.

For we that are in this tabernacle DO GROAN, BEING BURDENED: not for that we would be unclothed, but clothed upon, that mortality might be swallowed up of life.

—2 Corinthians 5:1-4

Apparently, it seems like it is saying that when we die, we will have a spiritual body. But I do not believe that this is the meaning of this word, since we do not have to groan in order to have an eternal, spiritual body. We already have one.

For me, it is talking here about something incredibly deep and worthy of consideration.

These are some clothes that Paul himself has to groan with anguish in order for them to be formed. It is a celestial dwelling that is manufactured in and upon us, that causes the mortal to be absorbed by life. It is the very presence of God that clothes the sons of the kingdom.

This is the heavenly dwelling that gave Peter the ability to walk upon water, pass through the walls of the jail with the angel, and that his shadow would heal the sick. It is the celestial, united with the earthly. These are the clothes that Adam wore in paradise, those that let him know he was clothed before God. It is the image of God formed again in us.

It is this union of the heavens and the earth, the earthly body united with the celestial habitation, that gives us access to see, to experience and to move ourselves within the two dimensions, that of the invisible kingdom and, of course, that of the natural world.

Paul had experiences in which he said, "I don't know whether in the body or outside of the body, I was caught away to paradise (paraphrased)." Paul understood something that he needed to obtain by groaning with anguish.

When Jesus speaks of this celestial dwelling in the human being, as I mentioned in Chapter 7, He also implies a process of seeking, and of deep love for God.

At that day ye shall know that I am in my Father, and ye in me, and I in you.

He that hath my commandments, and keepeth them, he it is that loveth me: and he that loveth me shall be loved of my Father, and I will love him, and WILL MANIFEST MYSELF TO HIM.

Judas saith unto him, not Iscariot, Lord, how is it that thou wilt manifest thyself unto us, and not unto the world?

Jesus answered and said unto him, If a man love me, he will keep my words: and my Father will love him, and we will come unto him, and MAKE OUR ABODE WITH HIM.

—John 14:20-23

We notice that here Jesus talks about a manifestation that is not in a generic form to the world, but to those that love Him. Here it is not referring to someone who said the sinner's prayer to receive Jesus as their Savior, but to those with changed hearts, who were obedient to the Word because they loved Jesus.

What Paul prayed with groans of anguish is that this manifestation would come upon those that love Jesus so that they would be clothed with the dwelling or abode of God upon mankind.

This celestial habitation is formed in us in the measure that we look at the glory of God with open face. This is the divine provision for us to be transformed into His image.

Once you enter into the kingdom of God, it begins to grow in you. Jesus said that the kingdom is like a grain of mustard seed, which a man took and planted in his field. It grew and became a large tree, and the birds of the heavens made their nests in its branches.

3. Anoint Your Eyes With Eye Salve That You Might See

This eye salve refers to the waters of life that come from intimate communion with the Spirit, and wash the eyes of our heart. This means that they are going to change the way we see things.

Saul of Tarsus was a man with a deep divine jealousy and a love for God that was willing to give all for Him. Nevertheless, his vision was twisted. The eyes of his understanding were blinded to perceive the designs of God. He could not grab hold of the will of God, or know it, because the eyes of his heart were seeing erroneously.

When he encountered the glory of God on the road to Damascus, and Jesus appeared to him with a shining light, his natural eyes were affected and he could not longer see. God wanted to give him new eyes, a new way of seeing things. He wanted his eyes to be blinded to the human, natural way of seeing, so he could see with God's eyes. Jesus said:

No man, when he hath lighted a candle, putteth it in a secret place, neither under a bushel, but on a candlestick, that they which come in may see the light.

—Luke 11:33

The light of the body is the eye: if therefore thine eye be single, thy whole body shall be full of light.

But if thine eye be evil, thy whole body shall be full of darkness. If therefore the light that is in thee be darkness, how great is that darkness!

—Matthew 6:22-23

If thy whole body therefore be full of light, having no part dark, the whole shall be full of light, as when the bright shining of a candle doth give thee light.

—Luke 11:36

Here Jesus is not referring to external things that you see with your eyes, but to that which is inside of us that makes us perceive things in one way or another.

In the spiritual world, there exists a light that is darkness. It is the light that proceeds from death, and distorts all things. It is this dark shining that blinds the understanding so that we do not see as God sees.

Job describes this light, saying:

Before I go whence I shall not return, even to the land of darkness and the shadow of death;

A land of darkness, as darkness itself; and of the shadow of death, without any order, and where the light is as darkness.

—Job 10:21-22

This is the light that illumines the fleshly soul. The flesh is death and it is darkness. It is this deep darkness that is accumulating on the inside of the soul, dulling the understanding so that the light of the glory of Christ cannot shine. It blinds the eyes of the spirit and we cannot see God.

Jesus said:

Blessed are the pure in heart: for they shall see God.

—*Matthew 5:8*

The way in which our eyes are going to see, depends then on the purity of our heart. The pure heart and the kind eye are the ones that see as God sees. They are eyes of love; they are redemptive eyes, eyes that see according to truth and righteousness. The eyes of God do not look at external things, but to the things that are behind them. They do not look at the appearance of human beings, at the external form of their works, but at the essence, at the heart of man; at their motives, more than their actions.

Man sees in a structured way, according to what he has learned from life or from the scars in his heart. Man sees things in one way or another, according to his educational and doctrinal background. The narrower the way of thinking, the more square and inflexible his way of seeing and perceiving things will be. The less he has been exposed to loving and receiving love, the more rigid and intolerant he will be.

God sees in different levels and facets, and His thought is ample and full of possibilities, like the diffraction of light, because love and mercy are like that.

For example, when Saul persecuted the Church, the entire body of believers of his day saw him as the worst of mankind. But God saw him from different angles, because He loved him:

1.   On the one hand, he reprimanded him for his crimes and his persecution of believers.
2.   On the other hand, he was in wonder, and was moved by his zeal and faith.
3.   He loved Saul's boldness, diligence for learning, and his devotion to keeping the law.

While the entire Church hated him, God knew that all that horrible man needed was a touch to his eyes, and he would change the direction of his steps. That is why Jesus said:

> But many that are first shall be last; and the last shall be first.
>
> —*Matthew 19:30*

God does not see as men see. He is not dazzled with that which dazzles men. He does not judge with a human heart, but with righteous judgment.

The books in heaven are being written very differently from the monthly reports of the Church. One story might be printed in the popular Christian magazines, talking about the glory that fell when Reverend So And So preached. And in heaven, it might have been recorded something like this: "Your angels made Your glory descend, oh Father, when they were touched by the fervent heart of Your intercessor that cried out for You in Such And Such Church. And one angel asked another, 'Listen! And who is preaching?' 'I don't know, he was covered in darkness. I couldn't see him.'"

Maybe on the outside, we are successful people, or we feel like we are great ministers because we are popular, or because the people admire us. But God wants to show us how to see as He sees, that we would see and walk in truth as He conceives it to be, in the light of His eyes.

One example of this, is an experience that I had some time ago. I was in the city of Nuevo Laredo in Mexico. We were in the midst of an extraordinary presence of God in the convention where I was preaching with other servants, when the angel of the Lord descended, and he touched my forehead. At that moment, I fell to the floor, and my spirit was caught away to heaven. From above, the Lord showed me how He saw the service from His perspective.

I looked down and everything was seen as light and shadows. The people and the preacher were seen clearly. But the words, the thoughts and what happened was manifested in light of different colors and in dark shadows.

Richard Hays, who was preaching, was taking up the offering. I did not hear the words, but I saw the light that went out of his mouth. It was very beautiful.

Suddenly, a dark red shadow entered. It was a demon of greed and financial fear. The light that had begun to touch the heads of the people became hazy on many of them. Pastor Hays continued speaking, and the light that went out of him crumbled that spirit.

I observed attentively. Richard then said something. I don't know what, because I only saw lights; I didn't hear words. And all of the people raised their hands, holding their offerings. I then saw something that dumbfounded

me. From a few hands, very few, went forth rays of light
that arrived where I was with the Lord, but the offering
of all of the rest turned into a black smoke that spread out
from between the fingers of the people.

Maybe on earth the people thought they were offering
something great, but in the heavens, the offering given with
personal ambition, or with a wrong heart, doesn't even pass
through the ceiling.

We have to be sincere with ourselves and see further
than the external form of things, learning to see as God
sees. The Word says:

> Unto the pure all things are pure: but unto them that
> are defiled and unbelieving is nothing pure; but even
> their mind and conscience is defiled.
>
> —*Titus 1:15*

Unbelief, which produces a mind that cannot perceive or
enter into spiritual spheres, comes from corruption in the
area of the soul and also the spirit. Corruption is the result
of injury, a hurt in the heart that did not heal, but became
a decayed wound. This cauterizes the heart, closes it, and
makes it insensitive to certain or to all areas of the spirit.
The heart is the bond between the spirit and the conscience
of man.

Carnal ground, as we saw previously, is in darkness and
disorder. That is why a carnal heart cannot be a channel
for the pure light that comes from the Spirit, because all of
their circuits (to say it in some fashion) are in disarray and
are atrophied.

> But the natural man receiveth not the things of the
> Spirit of God: for they are foolishness unto him:

neither can he know them, because they are spiritually discerned.

—1 Corinthians 2:14

He also adds:

But as it is written, Eye hath not seen, nor ear heard,
neither have entered into the heart of man, the things
which God hath prepared for them that love him.

But God hath revealed them unto us by his Spirit: for
the Spirit searcheth all things, yea, the deep things of
God.

—1 Corinthians 2:9-10

There are people today that want to find human logic
in everything they hear from God. And if their intellect
cannot process it, because it seems crazy to them, then they
refute it as something that does not come from God.

God is revealing new things that sound strange, because
eye has not seen them, and ear has not heard them, and
they have not entered into the heart of man. But they come
from the depths of God.

This internal corruption, which unfortunately is still
in all of us, is the true, internal prison from which God
wants to liberate us. It is what holds us prisoner, in limited
thoughts, in a lack of faith. It is what makes us seek natural
solutions to our problems, when we have a kingdom in our
midst where everything is possible. It is what needs to be
consumed by the fire of the Spirit. It is what needs to be
renewed by the water of life, the eye salve of God, to make
us again docile and pure of heart.

Children are born, and their spirits, having recently left God, seek love everywhere. The only thing that a baby knows is that he left the womb of love and love is the only thing that satisfies him. Then, little by little, the world, pain, the rejection that we all live, construct walls of protection around his heart.

For some, the suffering caused by life's blows is so painful that, unconsciously, they withdraw within themselves. They decide in their hearts never again to feel the pain of not finding love, or of being rejected by those who they decided to love.

The heart becomes reduced in size and it becomes of stone. It becomes full of walls, built by decisions of self-protection, shyness and deep fear. Fear is the number one enemy of love. Fear is that which displaces love in order to take its place.

This is the corruption of the soul. This is what holds the soul of millions of people prisoner who cannot enter the supernatural kingdom of God.

It is necessary to be brave and open one's heart again. And it is going to hurt. Yes, this step hurts a lot, because you have to use a chisel in the rock and scrape it in order to heal the decayed wounds of the heart. And then you must allow God to renew it as the heart of a child.

Loving others is an ointment that heals the heart and you become as a little child, who believes all things, because love believes all things.

Without this purity, without this returning to first innocence, in which we believed everything, we cannot enter into the kingdom of God or see the Lord.

At that time Jesus answered and said, I thank thee, O
Father, Lord of heaven and earth, because thou hast
hid these things from the wise and prudent, and hast
revealed them unto babes.

—Matthew 18:3

The generation of light, the man child, the governing
Church, the one who sits with Jesus on His throne, is a
Church with a pure heart.

Ever since I understood this, it is with boldness that I
seek in my mind and in my heart the areas of corruption,
the areas where unbelief could stop me from taking certain
steps in the kingdom of God.

What God has for us in his kingdom is so great. He
said that greater things we would do, because He went to
the Father. This is the time in which all past generations
desired to live, but that God is giving to us.

10

THE DWELLINGS OF THE SPIRIT AND HEAVENLY PLACES

Understanding The Prophetic Realm

1. The Spiritual Man

God reveals to us a spiritual world through the Scriptures, and it is in the Scriptures that we can find the anchor and security we need in order to walk with confidence in that world that for some is so unfamiliar.

Nevertheless, this invisible realm, which is spiritual reality, must be experienced in order to be able to move within it. The kingdom of God must be a lived experience, from which we are able to extract all the riches of His glory. It is worthless to intellectually know everything that the great men of God in the Bible lived in the Spirit realm, if we cannot truly possess these things for ourselves.

It is wonderful to read that Ezekiel saw the expansion of glory and the cherubs that moved with it; but it is much more extraordinary when God permits us to see it with our own spiritual eyes.

It is fabulous to study that John was caught up to heaven, but even better to know that God can take us. Isn't that right?

This is entering the kingdom. Jesus said:

> Fear not, little flock; for it is your Father's good pleasure to give you the kingdom.
>
> —*Luke 12:32*

> My kingdom is not of this world...as I am not of this world, neither are you of this world.
>
> —*John 18:36*

God wants us to stop thinking as earthly beings, limited to this existential plane. He wants us to think like celestial beings, as people of the kingdom, as a chosen generation, royal priesthood, holy nation, a people acquired by God to announce His virtues, and everything that is part of the multifaceted gamut of God's power. To enter the dimensions of the spirit is to know Him personally. This is the fundamental essence of the prophetic arena.

> ... For the testimony of Jesus, the essence of all revealed truth, is the spirit of prophecy.
>
> —*Revelation 19:10b*
> *(Paraphrased)*

When we talk about "the prophetic," it does not refer to only speaking prophecies in church, but to everything that is in itself the invisible world.

We said before that we are spirits, that we live in a body, and that we communicate, feel, think, and operate in the natural world through the soul. We also said that every spirit has the total capacity of seeing, hearing, and experiencing the spiritual world. And we added that every spirit that has been joined with God has the total ability to see Him, hear Him and to move in Him.

Our spirit is composed of three main parts: intuition, conscience, and communion with God. It is in these three segments that we can receive different kinds of revelation, as well as enter into different regions or celestial places. When the Spirit of God comes upon us in His prophetic manifestation, He is going to reveal to us something concerning the kingdom of God. He is going to reveal Christ and He is going to give us understanding of the spiritual world in general.

This can be given at the intuition level, as a word, or a sensation, or a vague form of vision. In this case, it is not correct to say, "Thus says the Lord," as many have done due to habit, since this is very delicate, but rather to say, "I have a strong feeling that…" "I have the sensation that…"

At the conscience level, we are going to experience conviction of sin. There will be voices of warning when we are entering the wrong path, or there will be a deep feeling of peace and security upon walking the correct path.

At the communion level is where the gamut of possibilities is more diverse and complex. Here our level of revelation with Him is going to be determined, as well as the type of calling and gifts that God, in His mercy, wants to manifest in us.

2. Visions, Revelations, Ecstasies and Being Caught Away

It is at the communion level that we are going to experience the different levels of revelation.

a. Prophetic Impressions

These are, as the name indicates, impressions that come to our spirit. They can be very specific and hit the mark. However, they can be contaminated by our feelings, primarily, at the moment of interpretation. We cannot at these times either emphatically state, "Thus says the Lord."

b. Visions and Dreams

These are clear visions during which our spiritual eyes and ears see and hear in detail. They can come while we are awake and conscious, or through dreams while we sleep. In this type of prophetic manifestation, the conscience interacts with the communion, bringing discernment, in order to know the origin of what we are receiving.

The messages that come from God always will bring with them a sensation of righteousness, of peace, and of joy, even though what we are hearing or seeing might be a judgment or the warning of a catastrophe. (Note: This type of prophecy necessarily needs to be judged by prophetic or apostolic ministers.)

The visions will always come in the midst of a clear consciousness of the presence of God. When the devil is interfering with messages that are apparently prophetic, they always bring with them an aftertaste of disquiet, of fear, and the feeling that something does not sit well with our conscience.

c. Ecstasies and Parousias

In addition to these forms of prophetic revelation, we are going to have a deeper one that is the ecstasy. Our entire spiritual body participates in this experience. It goes beyond a vision. In this form, you enter the vision itself, as if you were placed within a movie. You are not simply an observer, but now you are a participant.

This is the case that we see, for example, when Peter sees the sheet with the animals on it:

> And he became very hungry, and would have eaten: but while they made ready, he fell into a trance,
>
> And saw heaven opened, and a certain vessel descending unto him, as it had been a great sheet knit at the four corners, and let down to the earth:
>
> Wherein were all manner of four footed beasts of the earth, and wild beasts, and creeping things, and fowls of the air.
>
> And there came a voice to him, Rise, Peter; kill, and eat.
>
> —*Acts 10:10-13*

We also have the case of the parousias, a Greek word used to speak of the appearance of Jesus Christ in the Old and New Testaments. This is the case of Paul on the road to Damascus, where Jesus appears to him in a shining light, revealing Himself to him as Lord.

d. Being Caught Away

This is the most extraordinary kingdom experience to which God is taking his chosen ones.

We said before that every spirit that is one with Jesus can hear Him, see Him, and experience the invisible kingdom of God. We also add that the heavens and the earth become one in Jesus. Therefore, everyone who is one with the Lord can also move in celestial dimensions as well as in earthly ones.

Jesus paid the price for us to be seated with Him in heavenly places. And this is not only a position of authority that we possess theologically. Everything that Jesus conquered for us is not automatic. We have to enter into possession of each truth.

For example, Jesus died for all sinners. This does not mean that everybody is already saved. Each person has to embrace the sacrifice of the cross and enter into the plan of salvation. This same thing happens when Jesus destroyed the empire of the devil through His death. This does not mean that there are no longer demons on the earth, or that we no longer need to wage spiritual warfare. Believers have to proclaim that victory to the powers of darkness and submit themselves to the lordship of Jesus Christ, until all of His enemies are made His footstool.

This same spiritual logic applies to the truth that "we are seated with Christ in heavenly places." The Lord won the battle for us, so that we could be in those positions of authority and revelation, but we must take possession of them.

Outside of salvation, which is by grace, everything else has a price tag that must be paid. And of course, truly having spiritual authority has one of the highest price tags.

Heavenly places are real. They are glorious dwellings of infinite revelation. It is the will of God that we enter them, that we be established there, and that we govern with Him from the heavens, while we live here on the earth.

God is opening the heavens in a surprising way. Heaven's doors are being revealed so that we may penetrate into this dimension as never before (because this has to do with the end times, not before). The man child is being caught up in many parts of the earth, to understand how heaven governs and to be able to reign with Jesus Christ in the same way.

Is this biblical? Yes! We see it many times in the Old Testament and even in the New, because the Lord said that he had better things prepared for us than for the cloud of witnesses that we see in the book of Hebrews chapter 11.

What is God telling us and how are we understanding it?

There are visions and revelations that cannot be given to the servants of God on the earth, but that they must be spiritually transported to heavenly places in order to receive what God wants to give them.

What does this mean?

We see the case of Ezekiel. He finds himself captive in Babylon, and God wants to reveal to him the glorious vision of His temple.

... In the fourteenth year after that the city was smitten, in the selfsame day the hand of the LORD was upon me, and brought me thither.

In the visions of God BROUGHT HE ME into the land of Israel, and set me upon a very high mountain, by which was as the frame of a city on the south.

And he brought me thither, and, behold, there was a man, whose appearance was like the appearance of brass, with a line of flax in his hand, and a measuring reed; and he stood in the gate.

And the man said unto me, Son of man, behold with thine eyes, and hear with thine ears, and set thine heart upon all that I shall show thee; FOR TO THE INTENT THAT I MIGHT SHOW THEM UNTO THEE ART THOU BROUGHT HITHER: declare all that thou seest to the house of Israel.

—*Ezekiel 40:1b-4*

Here the prophet was taken to the most important heavenly dwelling, "the temple of God." He did not go to the physical land of Israel, since that temple was never build there, but to the temple of God above this nation.

The visions, then, are revelations that come to us, and the heavenly places, are places to which we are taken, and where we are established, as we will see a little later.

In the case of John, he also finds himself in captivity on the isle of Patmos, and the Lord is going to give him the impressive revelation of this last book in the Bible. In this complex manifestation of the prophetic, John is going to have different experiences in the spirit. He is going to hear celestial sounds, he is going to see the magnificent parousia of Christ glorified. He is going to find himself with a great quantity of angelic visitations that, in many cases, will take him to different places in the spiritual world. And he will also be, like Ezekiel, caught away to the third heaven.

After this I looked, and, behold, a door was opened in heaven: and the first voice which I heard was as it were of a trumpet talking with me; which said,

COME UP HITHER, and I will show thee things which must be hereafter.

And immediately I was in the spirit; and, behold, a throne was set in heaven, and one sat on the throne.

—Revelation 4:1-2

And there came one of the seven angels which had the seven vials, and talked with me, saying unto me, COME HITHER; I WILL SHOW UNTO THEE the judgment of the great whore that sitteth upon many waters...

So he carried me away in the spirit into the wilderness...

—Revelation 17:1, 3a

We also see that Paul tells about similar experiences.

It is not expedient for me doubtless to glory. I will come to visions and revelations (this is in plural) of the Lord.

I knew a man in Christ above fourteen years ago, (whether in the body, I cannot tell; or whether out of the body, I cannot tell: God knoweth;) such an one caught up to the third heaven.

And I knew such a man, (whether in the body, or out of the body, I cannot tell: God knoweth;)

How that he was caught up into paradise, and heard unspeakable words, which it is not lawful for a man to utter.

—2 Corinthians 12:1-4

Paul was in the third heaven and was also in paradise, two different heavenly places. I think, upon studying in detail the Scriptures of this great apostle, that he lived many experiences that had to do with knowing heavenly places, the dwellings of the Spirit, and the dimensions of the invisible world of darkness.

Peter himself talks about Paul and of the wisdom that God gave him to understand the heavens and the things of God, and how some of these things are difficult to understand. He himself has an extraordinary experience in the dimensions of the Spirit while in prison about to be executed.

He finds himself in this extreme situation, when an angel appears in his cell and tells him to gird up his clothes because they are going to leave the prison.

We are going to see here the two realms, the celestial and the natural, operating at the same time, and how the power of the spiritual world undeniably affects the natural world.

And the angel said unto him, Gird thyself, and bind on thy sandals. And so he did. And he saith unto him, Cast thy garment about thee, and follow me.

And he went out, and followed him; and WIST NOT THAT IT WAS TRUE WHICH WAS DONE BY THE ANGEL; BUT THOUGHT HE SAW A VISION.

When they were past the first and the second ward, they came unto the iron gate that leadeth unto the city; which opened to them of his own accord: and they went out, and passed on through one street; and forthwith the angel departed from him.

And when Peter was COME TO HIMSELF, he said, Now I know of a surety, that the Lord hath sent his angel, and hath delivered me out of the hand of Herod, and from all the expectation of the people of the Jews.

—Acts 12:8-11

Peter came to himself because obviously he was in the dimension of the Spirit. During this entire process, he believes that he is having a vision of ecstasy in which he and the angel pass through the gates of the prison in a supernatural way. Differing from Paul's experience, who does not know if he is in the body our outside of the body, here the experience is clearly in the body.

What is occurring here is that what is being lived in the spiritual world by Peter and the angel is reproducing itself in exact form in the natural world. The two dimensions are in operation at the same time. The Spirit of God has the power to invade all matter, and to move it from one place to another, even passing through walls, gates, or a mass of people, as Jesus did.

And rose up, and thrust him out of the city, and led him unto the brow of the hill whereon their city was built, that they might cast him down headlong.

But HE PASSING THROUGH THE MIDST OF THEM went his way,

—Luke 4:29-30

Believe me, Jesus did not push his way through the crowd here. There was just Himself against an irrational multitude who wanted to kill Him.

This same thing happened to Philip, when he preached to the eunuch on the road that goes to Gaza.

And when they were come up out of the water, the Spirit of the Lord caught away Philip, that the eunuch saw him no more: and he went on his way rejoicing.

But Philip was found at Azotus: and passing through he preached in all the cities, till he came to Caesarea.
                                                    —*Acts 8:39-40*

This is moving in the kingdom of God. This is for us today and we are already living it.

The revelation began to come to me while I was in the city of Aguascalientes, Mexico, preaching a conference of spiritual warfare with Brother Roberto Avila of Guatemala. The last night of the convention, the cloud of God's glory enveloped us on every side. We (the preachers) decided to leave by the back door, in order not to interrupt the Spirit that was manifesting Himself among all the people. Upon arriving at a little room just before the exit, we stopped to wait for the event coordinator. As we waited, Roberto began to feel extremely warm, and he grabbed his chest, as someone would who is having a heart attack. And, without saying a word, he fell to the floor, as if he were dead.

At that moment, an angel appeared before me. And, putting his hand upon my shoulder, he said, "Don't be afraid; he is being taken to heaven, but he will return shortly." I got in front of him so no one would touch him, and I told the others what the angel had told me. Soon, Roberto returned, and he told us his glorious experience.

This event began to turn over in my head, and it was soon afterwards that God would take me to heaven for the first time. The Spirit revealed how truly the blood of Jesus opened access to the throne of God, not only so that our prayers arrive to Him and we obtain mercy, but so that our spirit, which is one with Him, arrives literally before His presence in celestial dimensions.

God then began to take me many times before His throne and to reveal to me many things. Some of them are in this book, and I will have another opportunity to write about others, if God allows me to.

On one occasion, the Lord gave the order to four prophets to go to have an encounter with Him in the desert of New Mexico. During those six days, we fasted. The Lord opened to us the spiritual world in an extraordinary way. We were caught away several times and one of them was very special.

We had been in intense worship, when suddenly our spirits were taken before an enormous door in the heavens. All of us shared this experience, which permitted us to see one another, as if we were on the earth. We could also communicate among ourselves and our voices could be heard in both dimensions.

The figure of two beings similar to gigantic lions stood watch at the gate. Then we heard a voice that said to us, "There are places which only my bride is permitted to enter, and in a cooperative way." Suddenly, the door opened and a road of gold began to unfold as a carpet before us. The passage led to a place above the throne of God. And above it other places were visible, but whose access was closed to us at that moment.

Then a man appeared with the appearance of the Son of man, and, under His feet, everything began to become transparent, and a new place became visible. In this place, we could see kingdoms and impressive structures, but all of them were dark and complex.

We were awe struck as we saw all of this, when He said, "This is the place of wisdom. In this place, everything is revealed and everything comes to light. I have brought you here due to the battle that you are going to face against the ruler of darkness that is named "the queen of heaven," the great city that rules over the nations of the earth. This battle has to be fought from this place in the heavens. Here, none of the princes of the world have access to see or to understand. From here I will teach you to fight in a determinant and effective manner, and here you will be hidden from the fires of the enemy. I will bring you here as many times as is necessary. You only have to request it. I will also bring many others, those who are ready to fight here."

Since that day it has been wonderful. God has brought us to that place many times in order to see from there the structures of the kingdom of darkness. From celestial places, the locations of the devil's power, as well as his areas of weakness, become very clear. We have seen so many millions of angels assigned for battles to come, at all levels of hierarchy.

That day, God also showed us different doors in the heavens and how they opened at determined times, and then closed and then again opened. Some were eternally determined and others opened due to the prayer of the saints.

There are also roads that unite all of the angelic activity between the heavens and the earth.

I will even make a way in the wilderness, and rivers in the desert.

—*Isaiah 43:19b*

This is a prophecy in the natural, but also in the spiritual.

This is how Jacob saw it in Bethel:

And he dreamed, and behold a ladder set up on the earth, and the top of it reached to heaven: and behold the angels of God ascending and descending on it.

And, behold, the LORD stood above it...

And Jacob awaked out of his sleep, and he said, Surely the LORD is in this place; and I knew it not.

And he was afraid, and said, How dreadful is this place! This is none other but the house of God, and this is the gate of heaven.

—Genesis 28:12-13a, 16-17

Bethel was known from then on as a place where God manifested Himself (Genesis 31:13).

Ezekiel also found himself with a place like this near the Chebar River, where God showed him the open heaven, and this originated a series of powerful experiences with the glory of God. The prophet knew that that place was special, because he returned to it frequently, and a number of his ecstasies occurred at this place.

Patmos is another of these places. John wrote Revelation, not through only one visitation, but through having been caught away a series of times. The majority of these spiritual transports were not in the body, but in the spirit. And these occurred in a cave that was found up in a large mountain on the island. Today there is a small Orthodox Church there which is part of a monastery, but all around are virgin forests where you can go to pray. When I was there, the first thing that I noticed was that the door of heaven that God opened for John is still open. It was from there that I was carried away during seven days of ecstasy, four of which were inside the heart of God, as I related in a previous chapter.

Throughout the history of great revivals, God has opened doors in the heavens that have not yet closed. The same thing happens in places where the prayer of men and women of God have touched the heavens and they have opened.

David said:

> Lift up your heads, O ye gates; and be ye lift up, ye everlasting doors; and the King of glory shall come in.
>
> —*Psalms 24:7*

There are places upon the earth where God has established doors for His presence to manifest in extraordinary ways, and where He can summon someone to come up to the heavens. Various mountains in the Old Testament were doors of heaven, such as Mount Moriah, where Abraham took his son Isaac in order to sacrifice him. And later, David used it to establish there the Ark of the Covenant. Mount Zion of course, Mount Sinai, Mount Carmel, where God made fire from heaven descend through Elijah, Mount Tabor, where Jesus was transfigured. The doors of heaven were open near the Jordan, where Joshua passed over on dry land, and then where Elijah was caught away, body and all.

The doors of heaven unite the two dimensions, heaven and earth, so that the kingdom of God is supernaturally manifest among us.

Now, Jesus said, "I AM THE DOOR." This means that, in Him, we can arrive at heaven, not only after death, but now. The blood of Jesus literally opened that which separated the two dimensions. And He is still doing it. When we understand this, we can open the doors of heaven through the blood of Jesus in any place of the earth and the heavens will open and every manifestation of the celestial will be seen upon the earth.

We have to change our passive prayers that are simply hoping that God will do things, when in reality He gave us the authority to do them.

Begin to truly pray. Honor the name of the Lord. Cry out for the heavens to open, for His kingdom to come, and for His will to be done, and you will see what will begin to happen. (The greater the power and anointing, the greater the result.) And don't be surprised if it is said to some (those chosen by Him), "COME UP HITHER."

Paul, who was little understood in some of his writings, spoke of this possibility of being taken to spiritual dimensions with the Lord, not only in the experience of being caught away, but as something that he also had experienced on more than one occasion.

He says in his second epistle to the Corinthians, after talking about the celestial dwelling (about which we have already spoken):

Therefore we are always confident, knowing that, whilst we are at home in the body, we are absent from the Lord:

(For we walk by faith, not by sight:)

We are confident, I say, and willing rather to be absent from the body, and to be present with the Lord.

Wherefore we labour, that, whether present or absent, we may be accepted of him.

—*2 Corinthians 5:6-9*

Now, Paul does not think at any time that while we are in this life, we are absent from the Lord. He himself said that in Him we move, and live, and have our being. He also knows with certainty that Jesus is coming to dwell in the life of the true believer. Then here it is not talking about life after death, but of moving in the dimensions of the Spirit, of entering into those places of His presence, to heavenly places.

In this passage, he uses the words, "we may be accepted of Him." Where? In the body or outside of the body? If he were referring to when we die and arrive in heaven, he would not use the words, "be accepted of Him," because we would have already entered heaven. After this life, you are not going to labor to be accepted of Him, because, due to the righteousness of Christ, you are going to be completely accepted. Then the word "labor" is only valid while the option exists to fail or not to be acceptable.

Jesus tried to create a supernatural Church that would move, not only in the same way that He did on the earth, but that would do even greater things because He went to the Father.

"Greater things" means a much more powerful life than the one He lived. He said:

Nevertheless I tell you the truth; It is expedient for you that I go away...

—*John 16:7a*

Why? Because by the Spirit we would have access to the kingdom of God.

In this dispensation, in which God is revealing the dimensions of the Spirit in an extraordinary way, He is allowing us to know what heavenly places means. Heaven is not an enormous plane, full of clouds, with the throne of God in the middle, and with angels worshipping Him all over the place. Heaven is composed of different places. These places are manifested in different spiritual planes, and each one reveals something different about God.

We must understand that the Father is not a white-bearded man, seated on a throne. God is the greatest and most diverse gamut of attributes, of unspeakable and unsearchable truths.

God presents Himself and manifests Himself in a different form, according to the attribute or the part of His being that He wants to reveal at a determined moment. God does not have only one face; Jesus doesn't either.

Daniel saw Him as an Ancient of Days. Ezekiel saw Him as an expanse of fire; John, as One similar to the Son of man; Joshua, as a Man of War. Jacob saw Him face to face.

Moses saw Him in different ways. He spoke with God face to face, however, it is apparent that He looked somewhat different when the Lord showed Moses His glory. He had to put Moses into a cleft of the rock so he wouldn't die. This was a much stronger experience than conversing face to face.

In this passage, God says to Moses:

… Thou canst not see my face: for there shall no man see me, and live.

—*Exodus 33:20*

Now, the question is how was it that God spoke to Moses face to face (Exodus 33:11), but in this passage it says that if he looks at God's face, he will die? The answer is that God has different faces, and there is one that is so terrible due to the relation with the glory that it has, that no one can see it, and live. God then decides to conjugate the two dimensions so that His servant can live this experience.

> And the LORD said, Behold, there is A PLACE BY ME, and thou shalt stand upon a rock:
> *—Exodus 33:21*

Here we see two places, one celestial (by Me) and the other natural (a rock). Now, something very strong must have manifested itself when Jehovah pronounced His Name and all His goodness passed before Moses. It was so strong that Moses had to hide. Today, that glory is accessible, because the place where he hid is Jesus.

Sometimes God has allowed me to experience different manifestations of His Name when He pronounces it before me. His face changes from one face to another. It is like a sequence of visions, all different and wonderful, that manifest themselves when He makes His name resound.

It is a serious error when we try to imagine God.

> Thou shalt not make unto thee any graven image, or any likeness of any thing that is in heaven above...
> *—Exodus 20:4a*

He must be perceived in the spirit.

If the men of God had these experiences in the Old Testament, how much greater will they not be for us, who have Christ in us and we are one with Him.

The truth is very clear and simple. Open your spirit and receive it. If the heavens and the earth are one in Christ Jesus, and you are one spirit with Him, the heavens and the earth are one with you, then you can see and experience all that there is in heaven through Jesus.

Heaven is full of wonderful things, in which we must be established. This means taking the ability that Jesus gave us of entering into these things, seat us there, and make them our own.

It is not automatic, just like taking possession of our inheritance. The door was opened by Jesus, but we must pass through to the other side and take possession of that which He conquered for us.

The Son of God spoke of some of these places. He said:

In my Father's house are many mansions: if it were not so, I would have told you. I go to prepare a place for you.

And if I go and prepare a place for you, I will come again, and receive you unto myself; that where I am, there ye may be also.

And whither I go ye know, and the way ye know.
—John 14:2-4

He not only prepared the way for us after we die. Otherwise, what difference would it make uniting the heavens and the earth? If it says, "You know the way," (present tense), it is referring to something that He has already shown them about His kingdom and its supernatural character.

There are very glorious places, such as "the place of understanding." In this place, all of the mysteries of science are found that have been revealed to man. There is a place inside there where all of the languages of the earth are found and where you can literally move them from the invisible world to the visible.

God has had me penetrate this place several times, and there I have received English and 80% of the French and Portuguese that I know. One day, God allowed me to give a teaching in Italian, because the brothers forgot to bring an interpreter. I translated for one of my companions of spiritual warfare all of the information about spiritual mapping that they were giving us in Turkish.

The Lord talks to Job about this place, and He asks him:

> Whence then cometh wisdom? And where is the place of understanding?...
>
> God understandeth the way thereof, and he knoweth the place thereof.
>
> —Job 28:20 and 23

He also inquires:

> Where is the way where light dwelleth? And as for darkness, where is the place thereof,
>
> That thou shouldest take it to the bound thereof, and that thou shouldest know the paths to the house thereof?
>
> —Job 38:19-20

In this dwelling of light, the greatest power of truth is found. There, everything is transparent, and nothing can be hidden. Truth is the purest light. God establishes you here when you are willing to walk in the most absolute transparency, speaking the truth at any cost. Here the "white lies" of the masked religious people do not fit. Your voice begins to operate from this place, and it has impact that converts the soul. The power of truth puts down every argument, when it is spoken from a celestial position.

The price of establishing yourself in this place is very high. It requires deep levels of cross, and the total destruction of your reputation. Here, even the minutest self-justification or self-protection cannot enter. It is a place that exposes you continually. What is inside there, is consuming fire, but fire from which you come out as polished brass.

Here, theologies and norms of men are undone, in order for them to be shown for what they are, not as the religious people say they are. In this place, your eyes are changed in order to know how the heavens see and not how men see. Everything spectacular about the methods of men becomes shadow and abominable in this place. Here there are hidden rooms of infinite revelation, unspeakable things, as Paul said.

Another wonderful place is paradise, where you can eat the leaves of the tree of life and be healed. This tree contains everything that restoration and healing imply. It is as the Prophet Joel saw it, when he saw the generation that could not be conquered:

> ...As the morning spread upon the mountains: a great people and a strong; there hath not been ever the like, neither shall be any more after it, even to the years of many generations.
>
> A fire devoureth before them; and behind them a flame burneth: the land is as the garden of Eden before them, and behind them a desolate wilderness; yea, and nothing shall escape them.
>
> —Joel 2:2b-3

There are fountains and lakes of peace there, where God makes the soul to rest, as it says in Psalms 23.

The celestial universe is so vast that whole encyclopedias would not be enough to describe it. But the heavens are open for you, in Jesus Christ. I have only begun to enter the thresholds of extraordinary things, and my desire is to extend myself even further forward, to see if I succeed in apprehending that for which I was apprehended.

My most fervent prayer is that God raise a generation that knows His glory, that every person who has come to Jesus would be free of his earthly, limited understanding.

No one who lights a light, hides it under a basket, said the Lord. But this is what we have done.

Oh, we have enclosed ourselves in veils, so thick with religiosity, of a mental, ineffective Christianity, when God gave us the most powerful dimensions of His kingdom.

We live proclaiming things we don't even understand. We make earthly, so many supernatural truths that God gave us, because it is easier to be of the earth and to be in control of your world, than to be supernatural and have God be in control of your world.

I pray to God that these pages awaken a thirst and an unquenchable hunger for God and that you may know Him in the deep dimensions that He has for you.

I bow my knees so that

The eyes of your understanding being enlightened; that ye may know what is the hope of his calling, and what THE RICHES OF THE GLORY OF HIS INHERITANCE IN THE SAINTS.

—*Ephesians 1:18*

End